fearless

"Corbitt has something important to say to you about putting God first and foremost in your life, even in the most surprising circumstances."

Elizabeth Scalia
US editor-in-chief of *Aleteia* and author of *Strange Gods*

"Absolutely outstanding! Sonja Corbitt will lead you with practical wisdom, the sword of scripture, and the power of the Holy Spirit to help you to overcome sin and live a life of fearless love. You must read this book!"

Rev. Larry Richards
Author of *Be a Man!* and *Surrender!:*
The Life-Changing Power of Doing God's Will

"Sonja Corbitt tackles everyday spiritual battles with wit, wisdom, and the word of God. Rich with personal examples and insights, *Fearless* is a down-to-earth primer on spiritual warfare. I recommend its practical approach for anyone who wants to learn to confront the lies and lures of the devil before they take root, and live in the freedom and love of Christ."

Sarah Christmyer
Codeveloper and author
The Great Adventure Catholic Bible Study Program

CONQUER
YOUR
DEMONS
AND LOVE WITH
ABANDON

fearless

A Catholic Woman's Guide to Spiritual Warfare

Sonja Corbitt

AVE MARIA PRESS AVE Notre Dame, Indiana

Nihil Obstat: Rev. Jayd D. Neely, Censor Librorum

Imprimatur: Most Rev. David R. Choby, Bishop of Nashville

August 17, 2016

© 2016 by Sonja Corbitt

All rights reserved. No part of this book may be used or reproduced in any manner whatsoever, except in the case of reprints in the context of reviews, without written permission from Ave Maria Press®, Inc., P.O. Box 428, Notre Dame, IN 46556, 1-800-282-1865.

Founded in 1865, Ave Maria Press is a ministry of the United States Province of Holy Cross.

www.avemariapress.com

Paperback: ISBN-13 978-1-59471-693-5

E-book: ISBN-13 978-1-59471-694-2

Cover image © thinkstock.com

Cover and text design by Katherine Robinson.

Printed and bound in the United States of America.

Library of Congress Cataloging-in-Publication Data is available.

To

St. John of the Cross,

who taught me

to be fearless.

Contents

Introduction

The strangest week of my life began with the worst marital fight of twenty-three years. As he ranted at me, all I could get in edgewise was, "You're totally misunderstanding what I said!" His wild behavior was so weird and unlike him, in fact, that I dismissed it as a midlife issue, even while residual tension hung in the house.

The next day I got a letter from a former high school boyfriend (now married with children) who proclaimed his tender, eternal love for me and told me that he drives by my mother's house on holidays, trying to get a glimpse of me when he knows I'll be in town. He listed the names of several movies he watches when he remembers me. Bizarre, I thought, especially the timing. I started to grow uneasy.

The day after that, my husband's formerly abusive stepfather died of a sudden heart attack. He slumped over in a lawn chair after lighting a cigarette, keeling over while sitting in the yard watching my teenager mow his grass. All three onlookers—my son, his cousin with Down syndrome, and his grandmother—thought the man had fallen asleep. It was my son who discovered the truth, called the ambulance, and managed the crisis.

Although the man's relationship with my husband and the other adults was, shall we say, difficult, his grandchildren adored him. Both of my kids grieved deeply, along with my husband who was obviously

conflicted in his own emotions. My household was alter-
nately weeping and angry, and took their grief out on
me as the safest and closest target. I was afraid of emotional and spiritual depletion, exhausted by intervals of
consoling and then suddenly being required to absorb
and deflect provocations from every direction without
reacting. I was scared I would do something insensitive
or damaging.

The day after that funeral my own stepdad had a
massive heart attack. Because he's a father to me and
my husband's best friend (in his own words), our family's fear was like one of Tolkien's Balrogs raging up
from the pit and whipping all around us. There was
the shadow of death and immediate out-of-state travel
to my parents', during which I heard of my paternal
grandmother's death.

The day after her memorial, my son was attacked.
I couldn't believe it. What was going *on*?

I felt as though I were standing in the center of a
tornado while one shrieking wind of crisis after another
flew around and around me (literally, in the case of my
marital conflict). I envisioned myself standing in the
center, being battered and buffeted, while my arms were
flung upward to God and I repeated over and over,
"Jesus, I trust in you."

Late in the quagmire when my predominant fault
was finally provoked,[1] I remember asking God, "What in
the *hell* is going on?" And that was the point at which I
reached perfect clarity. I went straight to Confession and
Mass for extra fortitude and insight, and my spiritual
director confirmed my suspicion: there was a definite
spiritual component to all that was going on.

Before I became Catholic, when fear, conflict, or
difficult circumstances occurred, I was taught to automatically attribute them to attacks of the devil. I grew

paranoid that he was lurking around every corner. I spent a lot of time "rebuking him in the name of Jesus," but crappy stuff still happened, so I felt silly, realizing all my huffing and puffing was simply an attempt to gin up a sense of control and power rather than a rebuke with any real authority or power in it.

In the sense that the enemy's abiding desire is to seek out our points of weakness and exploit them, it is true that he is always present. But paranoia and fascination with spiritualism is also a temptation that can trap us in paralyzing fear, especially since pervasive personal sin and serious psychological disturbances do account for much of the sorry state of affairs around us. Oddly enough, discovering the history and ancient insights on spiritual warfare in the Church not only anchored me in the absolute reality and danger of a spiritual enemy, but also helped balance my paranoia and steeped me in determination.

The temptations of my super-tumultuous week came through people—my husband, my children, my own thoughts and fears, and a former romantic interest. But I knew not to turn on those people or to take any of the provocation personally. How did I know that?

What kept me steady during my exceptionally turbulent week was the absolute knowledge that I was being tempted. I was being tempted to sins of the mouth, sins of gluttonous self-medication, sins of impatience and feelings of discouragement, and sins of rebellion, fear, and emotional infidelity to my husband.

But *most importantly*, I understood (and my spiritual director confirmed) that I was being systematically worn down spiritually, mentally, emotionally, and physically so I would be vulnerable and more easily lured into giving up altogether—whether out of fear, discouragement or distraction—my plans for writing and teaching

a powerful study on spiritual warfare that was sched-
uled to begin the next week.

Fearless . . . Are You Ready?

Often the mention of spiritual warfare provokes
thoughts of the more scary and even seductive aspects
of what is typically considered in the realm of evil: exorcism; witchcraft; Satanism; séances; demonic attachment,
oppression, and possession; and so on. The Church is
full of two thousand years of wisdom, instruction, and
resources on these more serious degrees of spiritual warfare, also called extraordinary demonic activity. I have
left that approach and depth to her theologians and the
ordained.

We will certainly discuss the more fantastic mani-
festations of evil, but mostly as they arise in the context
of *ordinary* demonic activity: the typical spiritual warfare we all encounter in the trenches of dirty bathrooms,
squabbling children, irritable spouses, crazy schedules,
and overwhelming workloads that is all the more dangerous for its seeming harmlessness. So if the subject
of spiritual warfare threatens to scare you away, I hope
you will be at peace.

This practical approach has not been so widely dis-
cussed, and it is one the scriptures take and our last three
popes have called us to: "Man's life on Earth is warfare,"
says Pope Francis.[2] John Paul II asserted, "'Spiritual
combat' is another element of life which needs to be
taught anew and proposed once more to all Christians
today. It is a secret and interior art, an invisible struggle
in which [we] engage every day against the temptations,
the evil suggestions that the demon tries to plant in [our]
hearts."[3]

Satan and the demons may be implicated in all the disasters and woes of human life, as least as far as they are related to sin, but the biblical record makes it perfectly evident that Satan's power exists principally in his supreme ability to hide and deceive.

Sound frightening? It need not; I promise to show you why in the coming chapters. In fact, I am rubbing my hands together in anticipation! I believe these biblical principles are some of the most surprising and important you will ever learn and periodically review in your life with God.

We're going to spend our time together filling our minds and hearts with the power of truth so we can confront Satan's temptations and lies from the get-go, before they become entrenched and destructive: "If you continue in my word . . . you will know the truth, and the truth will make you free" (Jn 8:31–32), free from sin, anxiety, and fear. I am about to share with you all I have learned in the scriptures about following God from fear to love, and I will connect it all to our Catholic tradition, so you too can travel by this compass if you so choose.

Throughout part 1 we'll learn strategies to help us conquer our demons. First, we'll acknowledge the reality of the battle we are in and establish the root of our fear, depression, and anxiety. We'll investigate how the Bible ordinarily presents evil to us and how it discusses evil, because we want to know how evil comes against us in ways that cause profound fear, anxiety, and depression. Out of necessity, we will discuss it all linearly, but in reality we circle these subjects and approaches over and over throughout the book and throughout our lives, sometimes repeatedly in a single day! So it may be helpful to reread certain sections of *Fearless* several times as you go.

Then we'll start where the Bible begins its undressing of evil: at the beginning of all beginnings. We'll investigate the balance and beauty of God's plan, because without a precise view of perfection we cannot clearly recognize the evil of sin and are tempted to simply live with it and explain it away. We're going to explore the territory where the battles begin and are won: in the mind. We will discover practical strategies for recognizing and resisting temptation at the first opportunity and for wholeheartedly cooperating with God to reorder all that has become disordered through sin, our own and others'. We'll consider God's prescription for renewal and try it for ourselves.

After that, we're going to expose the prevailing after-sin attack on dignity that entrenches our fear, anxiety, and depression. We'll take a look at some of the scriptural designations and descriptions for Satan and how these descriptions are clues to understanding his nature. Through the names he is given throughout the Bible, we learn Satan's motives and surprising limitations. We'll explore our feelings of worthlessness and other deep, personal lies we believe that keep us slaves to fear. More importantly, we will wonder at the miracle of how we "live and move and have our being" in the tender arms of Love (Acts 17:28).

Next, we'll examine what really constitutes "evil" according to the scriptures through a study of Hebrews 3–4 and the wilderness wanderings and difficulties of the children of Israel. We'll connect their experiences to our own economic, religious, and political fears of the future. We'll spend a little time exploring end-times prophecy from the Church's historical perspective in the DVDs that accompany this book, because the scriptures and Fathers and mystics make it clear how and why "all shall be well, and all shall be well, all manner of thing shall be well."[4] For all time, fear will be conquered in truth. Love wins.

In part 2 we'll begin learning how to love with abandon. We're going to detail each "piece" of spiritual armor that God has provided to protect us from fear, anxiety, and depression. We'll explore the prayers of the saints as aids on our own journey. We'll make a handy list of helps for battling fear, anxiety, and depression.

Then, sometimes in order to get the clearest possible picture of something, one must look at its opposite. Through three mini-portraits, we're going to contemplate the mysterious coexistence of evil and holiness on earth, and the paradox of sin and grace in the people of God.

Finally, we'll watch as Satan pursues, encounters, and tempts Jesus in the wilderness. We'll discover what Jesus knows about resting fully in God's goodness and love, and exactly how to live and love with abandon.

Let's Do This

Whether you are reading *Fearless* on your own or as part of a group, this study is similar in its approach to my last book, *Unleashed*. And yet these meditative studies may be different from the fill-in-the-blank format you have done before.

When it comes to exploring the Bible, I believe there's room for all of us to feast on the Word. *Fearless* is full of scripture *and* study, so it's perfect for individuals *and* groups. Yet it is purposely brief out of respect for your time, and it is based on a topic we all struggle with in contemporary life. I'm not sure I know of a more relevant, maybe intimidating, subject for our times than the spiritual warfare of depression, anxiety, and fear. But

I also like to say I hope you find studying the scriptures with me less intimidating than spinach and maybe even as tasty as a cupcake.

I invite you now to consider marking your book as you read and to make notes in a journal of some sort as you go. Perhaps more importantly, I hope you will read with a Bible close by so you can underline or highlight verses that leap off the page at you, if you are amenable to doing so. These verses will be vital weapons in your arsenal from now on, and you will want to have them permanently handy. If you do not have a Bible, I recommend St. Benedict Press's *Revised Standard Version Catholic Edition* (RSVCE).* Because I reference it quite a bit, you might also read with the *Catechism of the Catholic Church* (identified as *CCC* in this book) nearby, especially if you are reading and studying as a group.

Expect each chapter to include the following:

- A Review: "Repetition is the mother of learning," as they say, so we spend some time revisiting each chapter in a concise way.

- An Invitation: This section applies the scriptures and the chapter to our own lives.

- A God Prompt: Here I offer specific ways to get personally and directly in touch with God.

---

* When reading and studying the Bible, it is helpful to compare different versions, because differences in translation contribute to our understanding of what the verses mean. Unless otherwise noted, I have relied on the *Revised Standard Version: Catholic Edition* in this book, but you will also find occasional quotations from the *Douay-Rheims Bible* (DRB), the *Good News Translation* (GNT), the *New American Bible, Revised Edition* (NABRE), the *New King James Version* (NKJV), and the *New Revised Standard Version* (NRSV).

The Invitation and God Prompt sections in *Fearless* are designed with both individuals and groups in mind, so a leader's guide is included in the back of the book just for you and your book club or Bible study group. A supplementary DVD series, also called *Fearless*, is also available on Amazon or http://www.biblestudyevangelista.com with additional information that is helpful for more in-depth personal exploration or group studies.[5]

The Bible promises that we can be free to love with abandon and live as *fearless* children of God! I'm going to share with you the methods that Satan uses to keep us all in slavery to sin, Satan, self, and sloth that I discovered in the Bible, and my own struggle from fear to love, for "there is no fear in love, but perfect love casts out fear" (1 Jn 4:18).

Now, let's begin; take my hand. What comes next are the most important things I can tell you about fear, anxiety, and depression. Together, we're going to look our fears squarely in the face and learn to love with abandon.

Introductory Group Questions

- As you study the cover and title of the book, what are your impressions? What are your thoughts on spiritual warfare? How do you struggle with fear?

- After you have read the introduction together, either think about privately or discuss aloud as a group the following questions. What do you hope to take away from this study? What do you want the Holy Spirit to do in your life?

- If you brought a Bible, thumb through it for a moment or two. Thinking back over your life, try to describe your relationship with scripture in one word.

- What, if anything, bothers you the most about the Bible? What makes you most uncomfortable about it? How do you hope or anticipate your relationship with scripture to change as you work through this book?

- Pray a closing Our Father, Hail Mary, and Glory Be together.

PART 1

CONQUER

YOUR

DEMONS

1

$\mathcal{A}$ Fearless Battle

Acknowledging the Enemy

I remember a time in my life when I lived in total fear. I was unsure of myself and my reality. I functioned in fear of my father, my future, and especially God. I feared being criticized, unseen, unloved, marginalized, and ridiculed. I worried and obsessed about failure, worthlessness, aloneness, disappointment, death, parenting my own children the way my father parented, and getting what I wanted and needed. I was anxious and terrified. I grew so sick of it.

Are you in a season or place of fear and anxiety, Dear One? Does fear of what lies ahead, of the future, hold you back from throwing yourself completely into the arms of God?

At the time I was a waitress at an upscale restaurant. The owners were tyrannical. One of them watched porn every shift in the office with the sound turned up and the television aimed toward the doorway. Also the executive chef, he roared into our faces with a drill sergeant's spit and rage when any dish returned from the dining room to the kitchen. Then he docked our hourly pay for the amount of the entrée. His wife skimmed the top from our credit card tips to the tune of hundreds of dollars a night and fired on the spot the two people I ever knew to question her lies, shrieking at the backs of their heads as they hurried out the door. Several times I discovered their young daughter cowering under clothed banquet tables after a parental onslaught.

The maître d' was a bright spot (I thought at the time) because he lived in the loft above the restaurant and threw wild parties for the staff and their friends with free booze and anything else anyone wanted. I experimented around and didn't make it home a couple of nights.

We weren't allowed to smoke while on the clock, but he would let us sneak up the spiral staircase to his apartment, out the back door into the alley, or into the empty ballrooms as long as we promised not to rat him out if we got caught. The night the owner caught me smoking in a darkened ballroom and grabbed me, I thought he was going to hurt me—and I was terrified of just what his porn-soaked brain might provoke him to do. To this day I'm not sure how I escaped.

We all hated the restaurant's owners, and because of my past with my father I was terrified of the chef. I followed the rules to a tee from that night on, mostly— except for the night a coworker and I climbed up to the roof of the Black Angus Pub in the wee hours after midnight and spray painted the G out of the name on the restaurant's sign.

My mom finally kicked me out of the house for repeatedly breaking curfew. I knew I needed to quit that job, but now I needed the money more than ever and I could no longer afford to. Anyway, I liked the work despite the rabid owners, and the money was spectacular, especially for a teenager. I was also reluctant to give up the parties and other "fun"—despite the fact that I was still attending church regularly, on my own.

As time went on, the partying and other sin I was involved in noodled my conscience, and I grew latently miserable at the constant inner conflict. But I couldn't see a future that wasn't the status quo. How would I support myself without that job? If I went "all in" with God, I'd have to give up all the fun I was having, even my boyfriend. I'd be bored. I'd be *alone*. And how could I find something elsewhere that made that much money?

The intelligent part of me wanted to ask God for help, but emotionally I was too scared. I knew my problems were my own fault and that I deserved where I was. The possible "new" seemed so unimaginable that I decided to stick with the miserable present. That was my modus operandi in every area of my life for years.

Perhaps one of the saddest realities in the Church today is the number of Christians who live every day with this type of paralyzing anxiety and fear. While desperately desiring to serve God fully, they are simply unable to move past some overwhelming obstacle. Sometimes the impediment is unidentified. But it is present like a huge weight on the chest that prevents a full, deep breath. Even "seasoned" Christians struggle with the temptation to fear, often because of the severity of their suffering or circumstances. Is this you, Dear One?

Doesn't fear trap us in a kind of agony of aimlessness coupled with a dominant self-interest? Surrounded and bombarded with data and information on every imaginable topic, it seems we have come to consider our depression, anxieties, and fears as issues of heredity, chemistry, biology, culture, psychology, geography, or modernity—but never as spirit. In agreement with Popes Paul VI and John Paul II, Pope Francis said,

"Maybe [Satan's] greatest achievement in these times has been to make us believe that he does not exist, and that all can be fixed on a purely human level."[1]

Yet spirit is real; in fact, spirit is the basis of all reality. Are we part human, part animal? Are we simply "human animals," as science tells us? If so, what role does human spirit play, then, in our daily existence?

Try thinking about your own spirit in terms of its moral, fluid, nonstatic, immeasurable existence. Close your eyes and imagine yourself without your body. What does your soul "look" like? Who *are* you?

Here's another way to look at it: Right this minute, today, can you pinpoint how holy you are? Imagine a scale of 1 to 100 percent. Isn't our "degree" of holiness in a constant state of movement toward one direction or the other? The realm of the spirit is changeable, intangible, and scientifically unquantifiable, yet it is just as "real" and in some ways even more important than the physical realm, for it is the realm of the intellect and the will that determines both our actions and our eternal destiny.

Fear is rooted in this spiritual realm. We're about to study the cosmic role that every soul occupies in time and history, but before we do, we'd better establish this firm foundation: at its deepest root, fear is a spiritual battle with a spiritual enemy.

From Fear to Faith

Here's a promise: "For God did not give us a spirit of *timidity* but a spirit of power and love and self-control" (2 Tm 1:7). I hope you'll claim this as your own promise from God, write it on a Post-it note and put it somewhere conspicuous, and then imprint it in permanent marker on the wall of your soul.

Depending on which translation of the Bible you use, the word *timidity* might also be rendered *cowardice* or *fear*. I like *fear* best. This verse is a promise. The spirit of fear does not come from God, Beloved.

Fear is not from God—ever.

By "fear" I do not mean the necessary, rational reaction to actual danger, or the simple emotion. And I do not mean the "fear of the Lord" spoken of in the Bible as a gift of the Holy Spirit (which we will explore later).[2] I mean abiding, paralyzing, oppressive fright and anxiety about a perceived future and its imagined threats: this is the working definition of the word that we will use throughout the book.

Isn't my imagination without wisdom a vicious tyrant? If, as scripture tells us, "God did not give us a spirit of timidity but a spirit of power and love and self-control" (2 Tm 1:7), then where does fear come from? The Bible says that, first and foremost, oppressive fear is a matter of spiritual warfare: "For we are not contending against flesh and blood, but against the principalities, against the powers, against the world rulers of this present darkness, against the spiritual hosts of wickedness in the heavenly places" (Eph 6:12).

Fear comes from the enemy: my enemy, your enemy, and God's enemy. In affirming the spiritual basis of my fear I am not blaming myself for struggling with it; I am simply acknowledging that I am somehow being manipulated. As St. Anthony said, "Fear not. 'Tis but an artifice of the Evil One to distract you."[3] What am I being distracted from? What am I really afraid of? If we cannot or will not acknowledge the reality of a spiritual battle and a spiritual enemy, we will be continually manipulated, paralyzed, and overcome by terrors. We will be spiritually sick, ineffective, and impotent. Our lives will be consumed in futility and fear (see Ps 78:33, NKJV).

Lord, Have Mercy!

Perhaps you find the idea of hell or the devil silly, both just superstitious beliefs of the past that have no validity in our day of science, psychology, and medicine. Maybe you think God is just as nice and polite as everybody else you know and would never be so poorly mannered as to consign anyone to hell. Possibly you associate the "wrath of God" with an error in taste or a bit of folklore at odds with modern progress and faith.

But heed the words of St. John Paul II, who asserted that "he who does not believe in the devil does not believe in the Gospel."[4]

The devil's existence is a matter of infallible revelation. Jesus himself taught the reality of a personal evil enemy and left us with a liberation prayer in the Our Father. Although almost always translated as "Deliver us from evil," that line literally means "Deliver us from the evil one," or "Deliver us from the person of Satan."

Pope Francis reminds us that "man's life on Earth is warfare."[5] St. John Paul II encourages us to take the challenge seriously: "'Spiritual combat' is another element of . . . life which needs to be taught anew and proposed once more to all Christians today. It is a secret and interior art, an invisible struggle in which [we] engage every day against the temptations, the evil suggestions that the demon tries to plant in [our] hearts."[6]

Some people worry that studying evil will bring it against us, but the enemy is already at work in our lives, whether we know or acknowledge it or not. "Be sober, be watchful. Your adversary the devil prowls around like a roaring lion, seeking some one to devour" (1 Pt 5:8). He surreptitiously plants evil seeds in our lives that choke out virtue if left to germinate (Mt 13:25). Understanding and actively resisting the enemy is absolutely imperative if we are to resist being led eternally away from God through fear, ignorance, or apathy.

The enemy, however, is both in us and outside of us. As St. Augustine said, "Never fight evil as though it were something that arose totally outside yourself."[7] I must know myself and the enemy of love in order to conquer fear.

The Enemy Without

Sun Tzu was a Chinese military general, strategist, and philosopher traditionally credited as the author of *The Art of War*, an important, ancient treatise on military tactics used by the CIA and US military academies. Sun Tzu said the primary strategy in any battle is to know one's enemy. He wrote, "If you know yourself but not the enemy, for every victory gained you will also suffer a defeat."[8]

The Bible says our enemy is the devil (1 Pt 5:8), an evil, objective reality according to the Church (*CCC*, 328). "Whatever the less discerning theologians may say, the devil, as far as Christian belief is concerned, is a puzzling but real, personal, and not merely symbolic presence. He is a powerful reality, a baneful super-human freedom directed against God's freedom,"[9] warned Pope Benedict XVI.

Scripture itself does not furnish systematic or comprehensive information regarding the exact nature of this impressive enemy. Most of what we know about Satan and demons from scripture is scattered and sometimes simply "hinted" at throughout the Bible, but two thousand years of patristic and theological Church history helps clarify what is there.

Designated in various ways that we'll explore in a later chapter, evil is pure angelic spirit, and so it is immortal (Lk 20:36) but not eternal (because angels are created beings). "'Angel' is the name of their office, not of their nature," stated St. Augustine. "The word 'angel' means *messenger*, an indication of their function," according to the *Catechism*. "Their nature is spirit" (*CCC*, 329). Because "the gifts and the call of God are irrevocable" (Rom 11:29), the fallen angels retain their created abilities but use them against us rather than to help us.

Like angels, the human soul is spirit, but the human soul does not become angelic after death, when it is separated from the body. The human person was created to be a fusion of body and soul; the human spirit is individual and personal, ordained to freely will, think, emote, desire, imagine, remember, and act by way of the physical senses. Humans seem to have been created as the "middle ground" between what is pure spirit (angels) and what is pure flesh (animals).

The separation of the body and soul that occurs at death, then, is an unnatural and temporary state, a condition that as Christians we believe will one day be corrected and restored to an even more glorious state through the redemptive work of Christ at the "resurrection of the body" we proclaim in our creed. Those in hell will be resurrected to eternal suffering in the body as well as the soul.

According to St. Thomas Aquinas, angelic power is superior to human power in its abilities because it is exclusively spirit, without any need for a body.[10] Angels freely think (Dn 9:21–22; 10:14; Rv 19:10), will (Jude 6; cf. 2 Pt 2:4), emote (1 Pt 1:12; Job 38:7), act, are self-aware, exercise power, and are immortal, indestructible, and relational, all without the use of the tool, the "flesh," we humans operate in (*CCC*, 330).

The most gifted writer could never do justice to the magnificent beauty, eclipsing intelligence, and surpassing power of an angel; every biblical person who saw one became terrified at their shocking magnificence. And angels are actually the lowest order and rank of the pure spirits! The Bible tells us the ascending ranks are archangels, principalities, powers, dominions, thrones, cherubim, and seraphim. Possibly an archangel is as far above an angel in perfections as an angel is above man.

Because angels are pure spirit, they are not bound by the physical laws that govern our spatial universe of time and matter (*CCC*, 330). Therefore, they possess the inherent ability to produce and manipulate phenomena in our sensory fields of perception and behavior, according to St. Thomas Aquinas, and they use the "mine field" of our accumulated sensory data (especially visual sensory data) to tempt us.[11] Fallen or evil angels have the skill, intelligence, and desire to attract human imagination to the fantastic, first as a distraction, and ultimately as the door to more serious evil and danger. We see this temptation illustrated in the fascination with "rebuking Satan" at every turn, where obsession with demonic "activity" can prevent our entertaining the possibility that sin, our own or someone else's, may be responsible for our circumstances.

At the other end of the spectrum, Ouija boards, tarot cards, psychics, mediums, and the paranormal distract us, darken spiritual clarity, and lead us into more grave sin. Because these activities are attempts to bypass God in knowing what we cannot otherwise naturally know, they are rebellion against Providence. Falsely presented as harmless experimenting, just another experience one should try, or as spiritually good and righteous, all such practices halt spiritual progress and ultimately cause spiritual death.

Although they seem fantastic and maybe mythical, angels are as real as the air we breathe. They are with us this very moment. Your guardian angel has been with you, tirelessly helping and guiding you, since birth (Mt 18:10). You've got an angel, right there next to you, just for you, right now.

The number of angels is unknown, but Daniel says "a thousand thousands served him, and ten thousand times ten thousand stood before him" (Dn 7:10), and the number of demons and fallen angels is "legion" (Mk 5:9). They have existed since the dawn of creation and have the benefit of millennia of experience with humanity. They are a formidable enemy. The great spiritualist Father John Hardon said, "The devil is not one person. The devil is an organized battalion of malice" who has formed a "mystical body of satan" on earth to mimic and oppose the mystical Body of Christ, the Church Militant.[12] Padre Pio said their number is more than all the men who have ever lived on the earth since Adam, so numerous that, if we could see them, they would block out the sun.[13]

However, Pope Benedict XVI assures us Satan's power is severely restricted: "He is not a second god."[14] God has limited the devil as in chains: "And the angels that did not keep their own position but left their proper dwelling have been kept by him in eternal chains in the deepest darkness until the judgment of the great day" (Jude 6; see also 2 Pt 2:4). The errant angels were cast down to roam "back and forth on the earth" (Job 1:7). In their malice, they will tempt humankind until the final judgment.

Furthermore, because God gave us unconditionally free will (*CCC*, 1730), an evil spirit cannot produce in us something that is against our will or that was not already there, either actively or potentially (Jas 1:14). They do not know the secrets of God (1 Cor 2:11), do not have particular knowledge of peoples' hearts (1 Kgs 8:39), and have no absolute foreknowledge of the future (Is 46:9–10), although they can predict reasonably well based on the past.

In fact, in the coming chapters we will uncover how surprisingly limited Satan really is. For now, that Providence should permit diabolical activity is a great mystery, but "we know that in everything God works for good with those who love him" (*CCC*, 395; Rom 8:28) and that, in the words of St. Augustine, "God judged it better to bring good out of evil than to suffer no evil to exist."[15]

Angels are the earliest works of God's creation known to us. We know they must have been created on or before the first "day" of creation, because Job indicates that the angels were eyewitnesses to the creation of the universe: "The morning stars sang together, and all the sons of God shouted for joy" when God "laid the foundation of the earth" (Job 38:4, 7). *Morning stars* and *sons of God* are literary terms for angels and have been interpreted so since the Septuagint ("all my angels," Job 38:7[16]).

Where Did the Devil and Demons Originate?

God has left the reason for the fallen angels' revolt mostly a mystery, but many theologians have argued that it involved blasphemy against the unique union of divinity with humanity in Christ. According to this premise, God gave the angels a preview of Jesus Incarnate as the Savior of the human race and commanded that they adore him—Jesus in all his human suffering, weakness, limitation, and humiliation.[17] The thinking goes that Lucifer—among the most gifted of all the angels—wanted union and worship privileges for himself but without humility. A thing cannot be one with another if the two are not alike, after all, and envy is the parody of aspiration.

Conscious of angels' supreme elevation, dignity, beauty, and magnificence above humans, Lucifer took offense and rebelled against worshiping or submitting to the "lowly" God-Man, Jesus. The book of Ezekiel laments, "You were the signet [seal] of perfection, full of wisdom and perfect in beauty . . . till iniquity was found in you" (Ez 28:12, 15).

Hell, voluntary separation from God, began. According to scripture and Church tradition, the devil and other demons are the "fallen angels" who turned away from God, saying, "We will not serve!" (CCC, 391; see also Wis 2:24; Is 14:12–15). Pope Francis said, "The Devil is a being that opted not to accept the plan of God. The masterpiece of the Lord is man; some angels did not accept it and they rebelled. The Devil is one of them."[18]

Can you see, then, why the elevation of what is comparatively "lowly" human flesh in Christ, and the coming resurrection and elevation of our own bodies above the angels (1 Cor 6:3), seems to especially motivate Satan to tempt us to sin in ways that degrade the body as much as possible, especially sexual sin since it perverts the flesh's miraculous life-giving intention?

Lucifer is another proper name for Satan that means *light bearer*. We do not know God's original purpose in creating Lucifer; speculative theology suggests that he may have been some sort of teacher whose role was "the signet of *perfection*," meaning *plan* or *pattern* (Ez 28:12). But in his pride he rejected the perfection of God's plan, placing himself in opposition to God and distorting his gifts, which are now twisted against us for evil rather than good.

The passage from Ezekiel also suggests that before the fall he may have had the role and capacity to test mankind in order to lift up and promote spiritual growth. St. Bridget of Sweden agrees: "Although the devil lost the dignity of his previous rank, he did not lose his knowledge which he possesses for the testing of the good and for his own confusion."[19]

We have established that angels were created with a supremely free will, unhindered by human limitation, and are therefore capable of love (*CCC*, 392). Because it is love that "fits" a spirit for the face-to-face sight of God and the eternal union with him that we call "heaven" (*CCC*, 1033), and because such love can only be proven through free and voluntary submission of the created will to him,[20] the angels "fell," fled, or were cast from his presence in heaven to the earth upon their rebellion: "Satan . . . was thrown down to the earth, and his angels were thrown down with him" (Rv 12:9). Jesus said, "I saw Satan fall like lightning from heaven" (Lk 10:18).

Later, after the sin of Adam, God would mysteriously give the more vulnerable human race a second chance through redemption. But there was no second chance for the fallen angels who, as Thomas Aquinas wrote in the *Summa Theologica*, "know all things at once: just as in heaven 'our thoughts will not be fleeting, going and returning from one thing to another, but we shall survey all our knowledge at the same time by one glance.'"[21] Without the limitation of a physical brain, the angels do not have to reason in steps. They have perfect intelligence and clarity, and they understood the consequences of sin to a degree that Adam never could have; there was no "temptation" as we normally understand it. So "it is the irrevocable character of their choice, and not a defect in the infinite divine mercy, that makes the angels' sin unforgivable. 'There is no repentance for the angels after their fall, just as there is no repentance for men after death'" (CCC, 393).

They are vigilant and hostile intelligences. Their wills are fixed, and there burns in them a complete, merciless, everlasting hatred for God and all men. This hatred is even more understandable in light of the apostolic Fathers' belief that God created the human race to replace fallen angels and the reality that we will one day judge fallen angels as victors against them in this life through Christ (1 Cor 6:3). "For," says Pope Paul VI, "by His incarnation the Son of God has united himself in some fashion with every man."[22]

Man is the only creature on earth that God has willed for his own sake to share his love (CCC, 356), so he gave us holy angels to help us reach the everlasting warmth of his bosom. But all the fallen angels' gifts, cleverness, and power are ceaselessly directed toward leading us into rebellion, alienation, sin, anguish, and despair in order that we might eternally forfeit that love. They only desire to deceive and corrupt us into turning away from God so that we die in a poor spiritual state and become their eternal slaves and victims. Their hatred is the result of not only envying but also hating the one who punishes them for their envy against him and those he loves.

The Rebellion: "In the Beginning ..."

When did this awful rebellion occur? Again, God has not revealed it explicitly, but some theologians believe it occurred within "moments" of their creation (we speak in terms of time, but Thomas Aquinas says we must think in terms of angels' successive mental acts[23]). The Fathers see a hint of that conclusion in the mysterious first verses of Genesis: "In the beginning God created the heavens and the earth. The earth was without form and void, and darkness was upon the face of the deep; and the Spirit of God was moving over the face of the waters" (Gn 1:1–2).

In verse 1, God creates. Then something awful happens (verse 2) before God fills creation with life. He then separates some sort of nonmaterial light and darkness (verse 4). In this passage Augustine and Aquinas see in the *darkness* and *light* the good and evil angels.[24] The actual roots and meanings of the language seem to indicate the same. The angelic rebellion, therefore, seems to have occurred almost immediately after their creation.

Still there's that pesky quotation from St. Augustine: "Never fight evil as though it were something that arose totally outside of yourself."[25] The great military strategist Sun Tzu agrees: "If you know the enemy and know yourself, you need not fear the results of a hundred battles. If you know yourself but not the enemy, for every victory gained you will also suffer a defeat. If you know neither the enemy nor yourself, you will succumb in every battle."[26]

The Enemy Within

Let no one say when he is tempted, "I am
tempted by God"; for God cannot be tempted
with evil and he himself tempts no one; but
each person is tempted when he is lured and
enticed by his own desire. Then desire when
it has conceived gives birth to sin; and sin
when it is full-grown brings forth death. Do
not be deceived, my beloved. (Jas 1:13–16)

Dear One, are you living in fear or pervasive sin simply
because you have neglected to even acknowledge the
battle? Are you conquered by old habits, over and over,
before you even realize it? Isn't that depressing? Has
anyone ever won a protracted fight without a strategy?
We'll talk a lot about specific strategies in the coming
chapters, but I'd like to offer some helps right out of the
chute since you're liable to experience what I call a pop
quiz this week.

Pop quizzes are God's invitation to practice what
he's teaching. Although they usually involve some
degree of difficulty and surprise, pop quizzes are not
punitive or negative; they are a great help in our formation, and we should thank God for them. Be aware, since
we are discussing temptation and spiritual warfare, that
you will likely experience some sort of strong temptation in the coming days. *Dear Lord, help us keep our eyes
open so we aren't caught off guard!*

A Smoking Battle

My first conscious, deliberate bout with spiritual battle began in my early twenties one morning during prayer with this verse: "Do you not know that your body is a temple of the Holy Spirit within you, which you have from God? . . . So glorify God in your body" (1 Cor 6:19–20). I knew that "the wages of sin is death" and that whatever destructive habit I allowed into my life and anything to which I was enslaved was ultimately a matter of sin (Rom 6:23).

All I could think about was how I invited cancer into my body with cigarettes, smoking up the Holy Spirit in a cloud of sin. I was cut to the heart and quit immediately, only I never made it through the day. Have you ever impulsively made such a resolution, only to fail immediately?

I tried several times but couldn't kick the habit. I also knew "I can't quit" was simply an excuse. The truth is I can do any holy thing I sincerely put my will to, because God says so: "Be holy, for I am holy" (1 Pt 1:16). And God would not tell me to do something that was impossible. So I got serious; I developed a strategy.

I identified the schedule of my habit: how long it took for a cigarette to wear off and the addiction to rear its ugly head. I researched quitting and nicotine addiction, the withdrawal symptoms, and how to mitigate them as much as possible. As an added incentive, I calculated how much money I spent annually on cigarettes and decided what I would buy to treat myself using that amount once I quit. I planned what I would do when my smoking buddies at work and my weekend drinking BFFs asked if I was coming with them, how I would respond, and what activity I would replace that

usual smoking time with. I searched for the pattern in
my temptation to smoke: what the mental and emotional
triggers were aside from the physical addiction.

I discovered it takes five days for the body to flush
nicotine completely away; the rest is a mental battle. I
imagined handing Jesus my last pack of cigarettes and
giving him my smoking habit for good. In short, I circled
and circled my habit in order to know it completely, to
know myself. I didn't tell a soul in case I failed again,
but I was ready to put my secret plan into place.

I timed my "quit day" with the last cigarette in my
last pack just before bed, so I could sleep the first nine
hours away. I wrote down Bible verses and kept them
handy because I knew from experience that during those
first couple of days I would think about smoking on a
minute-by-minute basis. The effort to resist the constant
onslaught was agony. I repeated the following verses to
myself over and over:

- "No temptation has overtaken you that is not common to man. God is faithful, and he will not let you
  be tempted beyond your strength, but with the temptation will also provide the way of escape, that you
  may be able to endure it" (1 Cor 10:13). "Where God
  closes a door, he always opens a window," as they
  say.

- "I can do all things in him who strengthens me" (Phil
  4:13).

- "For with God nothing will be impossible" (Lk 1:37).

- "*Fear not*, for I am with you, be not dismayed, for I
  am your God; I will strengthen you, I will help you,
  I will uphold you with my victorious right hand" (Is
  41:10, emphasis added).

As the intervals between temptations to smoke grew longer and longer, I sensed a growing strength and sure victory. I discovered I also had to quit drinking any alcohol whatsoever, because drinking made me want to smoke. I also took up a workout regime, because sucking copious amounts of oxygen into my abused lungs felt so invigorating that I never wanted to smoke again. Ha! Three birds with one stone! I am a nonsmoker today because I determined to obey, and in order to obey, I sought to know myself. That was a huge victory for me, and it made me confident for the grace of new ones.

Has it ever occurred to you that there is a spiritual component to the battle against addiction? Do you dismiss the idea of spiritual warfare where you see only psychological, societal, political, or physical issues?

St. John Paul II's reminder is so important: "'Spiritual combat' is another element of life which needs to be taught anew and proposed once more to all Christians today. It is a secret and interior art, an invisible struggle in which [we] engage every day against the temptations, the evil suggestions that the demon tries to plant in [our] hearts."[27]

Pope Benedict XVI goes so far as to call us all common exorcists! "The Christian can see that his task as exorcist must regain the importance it had when the faith was at the beginning. Of course the word 'exorcism' must not be understood here in its technical sense; it simply refers to the attitude of faith as a whole, which 'overcomes the world' and 'casts out' the prince of this world. In unity with Jesus, and with fear of God, the devil is easily defeated."[28]

Dear One, the activity of Satan in our lives is yoked to sin. If we conquer sin, either our own or the sins committed against us, we conquer Satan. Isn't confronting

sin the beginning of spiritual warfare, then? "Fear of the
LORD is the beginning of knowledge" because "by the
fear of the LORD a man avoids evil" (Prv 1:7, 16:6).

Some say that respect rather than fright or fear of
punishment is specifically meant here,[29] but childhood
wounds caused the two to be synonymous for me, so
that these verses were literally true: it was actual fear of
punishment that was the start of my relationship with
God, because the dread consequences led me by steps
out of sin and fear to wisdom, peace, and love. For those
of us with father or mother wounds that tangled up love
and fear for us from the beginning, these verses may
ring literally true. Some of us have to learn how to fear
our way to a proper understanding of love, and that's
what this book is about.

But some lack proper respect at all, and it's evident
in our apathy toward obedience. We say we believe God,
trust God, and follow God, but more often than not we
neglect to seriously, deliberately, and determinedly
attempt the elimination of sin in our lives or anything
else he asks of us. *It's too hard*, we think; *it's too big*, we
excuse, before we've even attempted a real strategy of
obedience. And that, Beloved, is the main strategy of
Satan against the faithful: temptation to give up.[30]

Padre Pio said, "Where there is no obedience there
is no virtue, where there is no virtue there is no good,
where there is no good there is no love, where there is no
love, there is no God, and where there is no God there is
no Paradise."[31] Fear rules, when love should have primary place in the Christian life. God forbid!

Waters of Life

"For you did not receive the spirit of slavery to fall back into fear, but you have received the spirit of sonship" (Rom 8:15). We receive the "spirit of sonship" that makes us children of God from Christ, from his victory over sin and evil through his cross and resurrection, and he conveys it to us through Baptism.

Just as God brought light and order to the primeval waters of chaos and made them capable of sustaining physical life, the Holy Spirit rests on our waters of Baptism as the generator of spiritual life (Jn 1:32–33, 3:5). The sea encompasses all the dim origins of life, the early Church Fathers say, elevating those ancient, natural waters—even in their shapelessness, disorganization, and gloominess—to a lofty state as the "seat" of the hovering Holy Spirit and the first "worthy vehicle" of his life-generating action.[32]

How much more powerful, then, is the spiritual life generated through him in Baptism! Water is a powerful scriptural instrument and symbol of spiritual life and vitality, such that the Easter liturgy is replete with biblical references to the freshness and vigor of the element as the agent of salvation and sanctification.

Exorcists say that during exorcism demons behave in ways that show they are defined and bound by the Catholic religious system. Did you know the Rite of Baptism contains a mini-exorcism? Did you also know that the blessing of the water in the font also contains a mini-exorcism so that it becomes "holy water"?

Through Baptism we have access to all the power and authority and privileges of Christ himself. Baptism into Christ is the basis of all true authority and the source of all spiritual strength. After that, we can be cleansed through sacramental Confession, said by actual exorcists in the Church to be more powerful than a ritual exorcism.[33] They tell us from experience that demons know all of our unconfessed sins, but whatever is confessed in the Catholic sacrament of Penance is unknowable by demons. All in-between, throughout our journey back to God from whose heart we were born, we are sanctified and cleansed by "the washing of water by the word" of Christ (Eph 5:26).

Have No Fear

"Do not fear," Padre Pio comforts. "Jesus is more powerful than all hell. At the invocation of his name every knee in heaven, on earth and in hell must bend before Jesus; this is a consolation for the good and terror for evil."[34] We need never fear the fallen angels, because Baptism has washed and purified us of all sin and all eternal punishment for sin. Nothing remains to prevent our entry into heaven: not Adam's sin, not personal sin, and not the eternal consequences of sin. All that's left is to wrestle with suffering, illness, death, frailty, and the tendency to sin, but none of that can harm those who do not consent to temptation to sin or despair but resist through the graces of Christ (CCC, 1263–64).

I have my guardian angel, a Church founded by Christ, the sacraments he instituted, and the full power of the scriptures, all meant to help me resist and to save me from the influence of all the devils of hell. Because of all that Jesus accomplished on our behalf, Satan no longer has any legitimate claim on us, as "children of light"—none whatsoever.

Sin is not a design flaw, a development error, a psychological weakness, a mistake, or an accident, Dear

One. Sin is a choice. And it will trap you in fear, anxiety, and depression, and ultimately destroy you. St. Paul says you never have to commit a single sin again, unless you choose to. Think about this for a moment: If you could finally be forever free of the habits that regularly leave you in a puddle of defeat, fear, guilt, and shame, wouldn't you want to? Through his glorious grace, Jesus has given us the power and authority to stop sinning. "Let not sin therefore reign in your mortal bodies, to make you obey their passions. . . . For *sin will have no dominion over you, since you are not under law but under grace*" (Rom 6:12, 14, emphasis added). Please read that sentence again—incredible!

Yet, Bishop Renato Boccardo says, "We are not asked to have shining armor to overcome Goliath, but simply to know how to choose a few smooth stones, the right ones, with the wisdom and courage of David."[35] What are the "few smooth stones, the right ones"?

The Sword of the Lord

"The word of God is living and active, sharper than any two-edged sword" (Heb 4:12), and that very sword proceeds from the mouth of Christ (Rv 1:16). From Genesis to Revelation God speaks, and it happens. He created all things and upholds all things "by his word of power" (Heb 1:3). His power has *word*; his Word has *power*. His Word is never empty: "So shall my word be that goes forth from my mouth; it shall not return to me empty, but it shall accomplish that which I intend, and prosper in the thing for which I sent it" (Is 55:11). The breath, meaning *spirit*, of his mouth is the only weapon strong enough to destroy the lawless one (2 Thes 2:8). One lifelong exorcist said that preaching and teaching the Word of God is even more powerful than Confession or exorcism, because "faith sprouts from the word of God" (see Rom 10:17).[36]

You may have grown annoyed by all the passages of scripture with which I peppered this chapter, and indeed the remainder of the book, but I am not sorry; they are your "smooth stones." Choose the ones that seem most useful to you and keep them close. We often perish and are overcome because we don't know how to fight better: "My people are destroyed for lack of knowledge" (Hos 4:6).

Did you know that the scriptures are the only offensive weapon the Bible explicitly prescribes in the battle against Satan? I intend to arm you to the hilt with verses until you can murmur them in your sleep, until they spring readily to mind in the midst of your battles. The sacraments and saints are some of the most powerful weapons in the spiritual arsenal, and we will talk about why in detail in the coming chapters, but they are only half the prescription: "For this reason, the Church has always venerated the Scriptures as she venerates the Lord's Body. She never ceases to present to the faithful the bread of life, taken from the one table of God's Word and Christ's Body" (CCC, 103).

The sacraments are available only once a week or once a day for most of us. What do we do in between? Doesn't the battle sometimes rage from second to second? We need the sword of the Lord to help us in the trenches when the enemy surrounds us and his shells are exploding everywhere and our hearts are near to fainting with fear, discouragement, anxiety, and defeat. Just as in Genesis, the Word of God in the sacraments and the scriptures is still the light he uses to bring the world and its fear, chaos, and anxiety—where life is unsupported—back into order and alignment where life can thrive. We must brandish scripture in a steady advance throughout our days.

With the Word of God we can "destroy arguments and every proud obstacle to the knowledge of God, and take every thought captive to obey Christ" (2 Cor 10:5), a practice also sometimes called "custody of the mind." Science agrees. In *Not Your Brain* by Jeffery Schwartz, the latest brain science confirms that the neuroelasticity in the human brain enables the creation and strengthening of new neural pathways when we refocus runaway, habitual, erroneous, anxious thoughts. This rewiring begins with truth, and truth is God's Word.

God's Word should be ever on the tongue. That's why we make the tiny crosses on our foreheads, our lips, and our hearts just before the Gospel at Mass. We are saying, "May your Word, Lord, be ever in my mind, on my lips, and in my heart."

Throughout this book, whenever you come to a passage of scripture, please pray it. Memorize it in the days to come. Absorb the words of these scriptures and saints. Attempt to glean their full meaning before moving on. In this way, the Bible will take root in our lives and help us become "more than conquerors" (Rom 8:37).

Let's Review

- *Fear is not of God*: "For God did not give us a spirit of fear but rather of power and love and self-control" (2 Tm 1:7).

- *Fear is a matter of spiritual warfare*: "We are not contending against flesh and blood, but against the principalities, against the powers, against the world rulers of this present darkness, against the spiritual hosts of wickedness in the heavenly places" (Eph 6:12).

- *Fear is an attack on love*: "There is no fear in love, but perfect love casts out fear . . . he who fears is not perfected in love" (1 Jn 4:18).

- *I acknowledge that, by virtue of my Baptism, I am in a spiritual battle with a spiritual enemy* whether I want to be or not: "Be watchful. Your adversary the devil prowls around like a roaring lion, seeking some one to devour" (1 Pt 5:8).

- *My worst enemy is not Satan but sin*: "The wages of sin is death, but the free gift of God is eternal life" (Rom 6:23).

- *Rebellion is the sin of Satan. When I say no to God, I fall into fear like Satan* who fell from the peace of heaven through rebellion.

- *Because rebellion is sin, rebellion introduces disorder that causes fear.*

- *Satan has no legitimate claim on me. Through the power of Christ, I never have to sin*: "Sin will have no dominion over you, since you are . . . under grace" (Rom 6:14).

- *God has given me his Word as an offensive weapon* in the battle against fear, sin, and temptation: "The word of God is living and active, sharper than any two-edged sword" (Heb 4:12). In him I am more than a conqueror (Rom 8:37).

An Invitation

As I experienced the power of the scriptures in overcoming temptation and sin, I became almost overwhelmed with thanksgiving for God's mercy in redeeming fallen man when he did not redeem fallen angels, and for the magnitude of the help he has provided for us. Indeed, Dear One, we are steeped in spiritual graces and surrounded by a great cloud of witnesses that stands by to help us (Heb 12:1) so that the only way not to make it to fearless love is simply not to try. Let's resolve not to live the same year eighty-nine times and call it a life.

God Prompt

This study is about fear. There may be a lot in your way right now, Dear One—a lot of fear, a lot of pain, and a lot of sin—but you don't have to keep living with it. Jesus made sure of that. But what if what you're looking for is not found but made?

As we saw in the account of angelic creation, rebellion (sin) produces a lack of order. A lack of order produces fear. And fear devours from the inside. Finding and fighting our way from fear to love requires brutal honesty with Christ about our rebellion and chaos. What in your life is in chaos and confusion? Maybe it was your "fault," maybe it was someone else's, but what has been wasted and ruined? What is devouring you? Maybe you want to talk to God about that now.

> *Lord, my heart is so heavy and broken over . . .*
>
> *I long for your touch in this area . . .*
>
> *Only you can bring order and light into the darkness here . . .*
>
> *Lord, I sense you are speaking to me about this particular area of my life . . .*
>
> *I want to be fearless, but I am being held back by . . .*
>
> *Lord, I confess that rebellion against you may have caused or contributed to my circumstances here . . .*
>
> *Lord, I need to know that your love for me is permanent and unconditional even during seasons when my life is not pleasing to you.* (Read 1 John

1:9, below. You may want to journal a prayer
response to God restating and receiving what
he is saying to you.)
I sense you want me to . . .

Has God spoken to you through this chapter about
some area of rebellion? Have you said, "No, I will not
serve," to him someplace, or, "No, I will not," or just
"No"?

Without trying to figure out *how* you're going to
get from no to yes right now, spend a few moments
(maybe the week too) meditating on the following verse
and asking God if there's some area of *no* he'd like you
to work with him on making *yes*. If you sense or know
there are many issues, ask him which is best to begin
with and listen for his answer as you meditate on the
verse below. Pay attention for as long as it takes, maybe
weeks, to hear his answer, and ask him to make himself clearly understood through prayer, circumstances,
other people, and so forth. But right now let's start by
emphasizing each word or phrase in turn until you have
emphasized them all, like this:

"*If* we confess our sins, he is faithful and just,
and will forgive our sins and cleanse us from all
unrighteousness" (1 Jn 1:9).

"If *we* confess our sins, he is faithful and just,
and will forgive our sins and cleanse us from all
unrighteousness" (1 Jn 1:9).

"If we *confess* our sins, he is faithful and just,
and will forgive our sins and cleanse us from all
unrighteousness" (1 Jn 1:9).

"If we confess *our* sins, he is faithful and just,
and will forgive our sins and cleanse us from all
unrighteousness" (1 Jn 1:9).

"If we confess our *sins*, he is faithful and just, and will forgive our sins and cleanse us from all unrighteousness" (1 Jn 1:9).

What do you need to do next? If you don't know, ask him and sit quietly for a few minutes. I love the promise of 1 John 1:9; it brings me great hope when I am trapped in sin of some sort and feel as if I can't find my way out or don't have the strength or the will, because it doesn't just mean that he will forgive the times we have sinned in a particular way, so we're clean to go out and probably mess up again. It means he will cleanse us of the sin: he will rid my life of the sin-habit completely if I trust him to and if I obey as he does so. What is God saying to you through this passage?

As you move forward into the coming week, I invite you to copy this verse and the scriptures in the Let's Review section and tape them up somewhere helpful. You might want to pray them back to God, knowing that the Holy Spirit is your helper in all that pertains to your spiritual house: "Be strong and of good courage, and do it. *Fear not*, be not dismayed; for the Lord God, even my God, is with you. He will not fail you or forsake you, until all the work for the service of *the house* of the Lord is finished (1 Chr 28:20, emphasis added).

Above all, Dear One, do not fear the evil snares of the enemy. In the end, he is powerless where a soul that is very dear to Jesus is concerned. Therefore, be at peace.

2

$\mathscr{F}$earless Reconnaissance

Unveiling the Strategy

Probably no one would say this out loud, or maybe even silently to herself, but sometimes I sin big on purpose. Maybe I'm tired. Maybe I'm hungry. Maybe I'm angry. Maybe the effort to resist seems to require more than I am at the moment. Maybe I'm weary of being "good" and want to let loose a little—or a lot.

As one blogger put it, "Sometimes I leave God behind to follow myself."[1] In my mind I see this leaving God as a little like what toddlers do when exploring: they run off to play away from parental home base, further and further each time, but always within sight and always returning as though some invisible tether reels them back in just when they begin to feel scared.

This idealistic view of my sin seems benign. The problem is, I always resist his presence in prayer or stop praying altogether when I leave God for myself. I'm sure he's *seen* me and is mad, sad, or gonna spank my butt. And if there's no prayer, there's no tether to God.

Disunity, scattering, especially separation from God, is always the devil's strategy.

In the previous chapter we found ourselves thrown into a battle for souls—our own and the souls of the people with whom we come into contact. We know that the fallen angels, from the moment they fell and were no longer capable of good, have thereafter and unto this day sought out of envy to tempt humans into sin and ultimate destruction. Because the battle is so fierce, involving all of time and creation, the Church calls us earth dwellers the Church Militant. Ultimately, we discovered that sin and rebellion inherently disorders what God has created, casting it all into fear. But *why* is this so?

In order to understand why, we must begin where the Bible begins its reconnaissance of fear and evil—at the beginning. Since, as we discovered in chapter 1, the most powerful and effective way to address fear is to bring the light of God's Word to bear on it, let's begin by looking at the first occurrence of the word *fear* in the scriptures, because we might learn to suspect that fear is simply a fig leaf.

Behold, It Was Very Good

We know the story of our genesis. Buried under such capital words as Garden of Eden, Paradise, the Fall, and Original Sin, we've heard it so often that the glory is near invisible and the tragedy has lost all sting. Maybe we should take a fresh look.

Maybe we should watch the tenderness, almost *wastefulness*, with which the matchless Other invents, shaping and structuring our spectacular universe out of nothing. Consider all those innumerable forms of personal expression in huge flocks, sprays, caches, and prairies, all pouring out of moments and matter: big bang and ocean canyon, sunrise and hurricane, acre upon brilliant acre of wild bluebells, breeching whale and whining gnat, iceberg and stalagmite, fern, redwood, and woolly mammoth—beauty that slams against our faces, unwilling to be ignored.

See him bend to sculpt wads of dirt into fragile human flesh and kiss, in the words of the great poet John Milton, "this new Favorite Of Heav'n, this Man of Clay,"[2] with the capacity to accept and embrace the divine breath. He becomes "a living soul" (Gn 2:7, DRB), a likeness of Holy God, Holy Mighty One, Holy Immortal One.

Notice him regard Adam's aloneness only so long as it takes to fully reveal his longing defect and to draw a hidden, priceless intimacy out of his startled ecstasy and rib. Do you see the wisdom of the first order, the circle of self-donation, the fruitful equality, and the mysterious face-to-face complementarity? She is born of him, so that he can be born of her. She is a "helper" or *battle partner*, "suitable" or "fit" for him, meaning his *opposite* or *complement* (Gn 2:18).

Together they are able to do something greater than either can do alone. Uniting with each other so closely as to become "one flesh," man and woman rediscover, so to speak, every time and in a special way, the mystery of creation. As John Paul II taught us so poetically in his soaring *Theology of the Body*, the physical and personal complementarity of man and woman, along with the "duality of a mysterious mutual attraction," reminds us that in the Garden where all is unblemished, "femininity finds itself, in a sense, in the presence of masculinity, while masculinity is confirmed through femininity."[3]

In a continuous halo of physical exchange that mimics the emotional, intellectual, and spiritual levels of relation between them—all of them transparent, self-giving, equal, and complementary too—they experience and incarnate the inner order and interpersonal meaning of that first circle of generous self-donation, loving equality, glorious complementarity, and exponential fruitfulness of the Holy Trinity from which they proceed.

As sublime as they are in the circle of one another and him, isn't it still shocking when he turns the whole stunning, pristine, cosmic work of art over to the stewardship of these low, newly made, plain human creatures? Why does he do something so seemingly irresponsible when he must know what will happen next? After all, it was the central plan for the Incarnation that caused the rebellious angels to fall.

Could it be that he is far more interested in experiencing Adam and Eve in relationship—witnessing their delight in him and one another and all the beauty he so tenderly invented, sculpted, and offered to them as gift—than in preserving the perfection of what he made?

Consider also the exactness of planetary position that produced a climate in which all life grew and flourished with no need of rain, hibernation, or garment; think of the flawless harmony among humanity, soil, and fanged beast that made for peaceable sharing and contribution to earth's bounty. Observe the transparent vulnerability and the intimate generosity between man and wife, depicted in the naked shamelessness in which they "knew" one another in the presence of their Creator. Completely fearless and utterly open with no duplicity or thing withheld, imagine them "knowing" God with similar intimacy on their daily "walk" with him through the Garden in the "cool of the day" (Gn 3:8). How poignant it was.

What happy, beautiful simplicity existed there. Every intellectual, spiritual, emotional, and physical need and relationship was met and maintained in perfect balance, and "it was very good" (Gn 1:31). The word *very* in this verse means *vehemently, utterly*. Everything in existence was ordered to, depending on, and experiencing God as vehement, utter life, even to the angels' songs and shouts of joy (Job 38:7). "And God saw everything that he had made, and behold, it was very good" (Gn 1:31).

Then all hell broke loose.

The Great Sorrow

Was it the union that draws life from her, as the poet Milton suggested in *Paradise Lost*? Was it "Conjugal love, than, which perhaps no bliss enjoyed by us excites his envy more,"[4] that brought the enemy against the woman in the serpent? Or perhaps, as John Paul II points out, it was because "God entrusted the human being to woman."[5] Whatever it was, the angel who was created for soaring music (Ez 28:13) but would only ever scuttle and snarl again, having irrevocably chosen the malicious path of fear and darkness, moved to snatch all of creation out of the bosom of the Giver down into the miry depths of his terror, shame, and despair.[6] Take careful note: the woman is his first object of interest, the one upon whom his active, envious hatred is first unleashed.

Like seeping, silent sarin gas with no odor to warn, the first noxious lie was released into the pristine atmosphere. The Giver of creation's plenitude—everything—was accused of selfishness. The first sin committed in the Garden was this devil's lie.

And it was said the fruit of the taking, opposite their current relationship of receiving, would be to know good and evil. But they already knew Good as intimately as it was possible to do so. "To know" in the scriptures means to have experiential knowledge of something or someone. Having flowed from Good himself, "it was very good" (Gn 1:31) in the Garden, and this goodness our first parents knew face-to-face and dearly well; they walked with him every afternoon. To *know* the random and frightening chaos of evil that proceeds from a lie would be the only fruit of the taking of that tree.

Consulting only her senses when the danger was physically undetectable, she surrendered her will and stepped out of the protection of community, reaching for the independence that untethers all of physical life from spiritual. She transferred it to her husband, and—in Milton's words—woe was unleashed: "Earth trembled from her entrails . . . sky lowered, and muttering thunder, wept some sad drops at completing the mortal sin."[7] In one breath, the breath of God expelled.

In whatever light we regard the fault of this unhappy pair, it is truly enormous. The principle was so straightforward and sensible, the lie so sly an assault and unfair a characterization of the true danger, and the suggestion that they should experience something more titillating than the bounty of what was already given so ungrateful and truly obscene in hindsight, that nothing but raw arrogance could have proposed their disobedience, and we must surely mark their sin down to a complete innocence of the existence or immediate presence of deceit and evil.

Because we, ourselves, never immediately experience and cannot fathom the full import and consequence of a single sin in our own lives, we have the awful apathy of habit to numb the truly cosmic tragedy of simple sin.

But look with me for a moment at the universal corruption that follows in the wake of this sin and the alarming change in the relationship Adam and Eve had shared so intimately with one another, with God, and with creation itself. Their ruin and that of posterity was clear, because stripped of the armor of original grace— that perfect clarity and power of reason over thought, memory, and will—they *knew* darkness and defenselessness where a moment before it had not existed. Everything and everyone was suddenly heaved into shocking terrors. All that had been in smooth harmony was now disjointed, frightening, jagged, sharp, and dangerous. Separated.

The glorious circle was broken. They were divided from one another by a "rift"; in Heather King's incisive words, "decreeing that henceforward, we would all be baffled, bewildered, longing to connect; all aching for each other and afraid of each other."[8] Now it's every man for himself, a brutal scuffle into role and rank. This awful, lonely separation from one another and God is felt as *fear* (Gn 3:10).

The Great Divorce

Finding themselves in a traumatic backwash of dread so great that their previously comfortable nudity is instantly disorienting and embarrassing, they cobble fig leaves together to cover from each other what they suddenly interpret is a threatening vulnerability, proving for the first time that when we choose independence over relationship we become dangerous to one another. Gone is their easy, selfless care for the other's good in generous service and mutual submission. They have lurched into a sharp struggle for power and dominance;

they are only too willing, now, to accuse one another, the serpent, and God.

What confusion must seize them as they remember what was and how terribly wrong this new "knowledge" is, their image of God now distorted into one of anger and jealousy for his prerogatives. Yet, was he really angry when the redemptive Incarnation was already planned, even before the fall of angelic hosts or earth's humanity? Is he anticipating, now, their reaction to his uninterrupted love even when they're "bad"? Dare I suggest his tenderness is even intensified in seeing them in this condition?

Yet, the familiar sound of him leisurely "walking in the garden in the cool of the day" elicits from them a new terror, such that they hide from the Giver for the first time. How sad it is when they avoid his company. A dreadful wound it is. These pitiful souls now lack the comfort and security of the grace relationship, which, of themselves, they will never regain. They haven't any idea how to anyway.

All that was unified and natural in the state of innocence is now a toxic mix of division and fear. There is a new enmity in the animal domain, so that it is hostile and alien. The earth itself, just hours ago entirely fruitful, is uncooperative, suffocating quietly on vines, weeds, and thistles. Have you ever thought of yourself as this intertwined with flora and fauna? As Pope Francis has stressed, the soil, the water, the air, the elements: "nothing in this world is indifferent to us."[9]

Frightfully patient, the dark dirt waits with yawning mouth to devour the flaccid flesh of man. The spirit will be utterly vanquished and separated from the body: death—that cold, dark disconnect—enters the world. Man has severed the relationship that tethers him to his last end. Because their souls will live forever, they must be thrust altogether from the sustaining womb of Eden, lest they also eat of the Tree of Life and "live" eternally condemned to the dark, fearful state of death.

The Spirit of Sin, to Divide and Conquer

St. Augustine says that "to prevent the sheep from seeking assistance by her cries, the wolf seizes her by the neck, and thus securely carries her away and devours her. The devil acts in a similar manner with the sheep of Jesus Christ. After having induced them to yield to sin, he seizes them by the throat that they may not confess their guilt, and thus he securely brings them to hell."[10]

St. Marcarius of Egypt once said sin is a spirit.[11] Tempting us to sin is Satan's only strategy because it is his only real power against us in separating us from God, from others, and from ourselves. Sin separates us from God because it untethers us from God's provision and guidance, and we are left to the terror and responsibility of our disorder and self-sufficiency.

Sin separates us from others, because it causes breaches in our important relationships that make intimacy and community difficult or impossible. Our sin affects others this way, and others' sin affects us this way.

Finally, sin separates us from ourselves because the conscience instinctively knows and tends toward God's law so that every sin makes my conscience suffer (Rom 1:18–21). Often pervasive fear and anxiety are the result of the war between my nagging conscience and my attempts to bury it under rationalizations, denial, and self-medication.[12] The conscience, as part of what makes me created in God's image, insists on truth, and fear foments in an assaulted conscience. Confess, Dear One; confess it all!

A Grave with Both Ends Kicked Out

In the same way that humans, who are lower than God, did not remain in God's higher will, their lower gift of the flesh no longer obeys their higher gifts of reason and will.[13] The soul's capacity to judge properly and control the body is diminished to the point of ruin through sin. I can't break the habit; I can't be selfless; I can't help myself; I can't suffer; I can't embrace death; I am a slave to sin (Jn 8:34). "I can will what is right, but I cannot do it. For I do not do the good I want, but the evil I do not want is what I do" (Rom 7:18–19).

Philosophy, psychology, and neuroscience all tell us that the body maps behavior like a car travels a dirt road. Each time the car travels the road, it becomes more worn, until the grooves are so deep that it cannot get out of the "beaten path" or travel any other way.

Since the soul and mind are located within the body and all sensory data enters through the body and is stored in the memory, all sin takes place in the body. Sin dulls the mind and senses by laying down ruts that train them to associate things in sinful ways. The next time I encounter that thing, the former association is automatically remembered in a way that makes it hard to see the thing as it really is and harder to resist. The deeper the ruts, the more frequent and serious the sin, and vice versa. In the end, isn't a rut simply a grave with both ends kicked out?

Sin—more than Satan—is the enemy of the soul. Satan is yoked to sin. His only power is his ability to convince us to sin—any sin. Just one sin is required,

since one leads to another, and like all things that proceed from a single seed, a single sin communicates
exponentially. Do people ever really know how their
personal sin affects those around them? After all, it was
a single sin that disrupted the entire cosmos, so that it is
all under "bondage to decay" with us (Rom 8:21).

"The exact transmission of Original Sin is a mystery"
(CCC, 404), but "sin came into the world through one
man [Adam as first and representative of all] and death
through sin, and so death spread to all men because all
men sinned" (Rom 5:12). Had Adam and Eve not fallen,
man would have never suffered fear and anxiety. For
this reason we can accurately say that fear is the result
of sin, either original or actual.

As Pope Francis's encyclical *Laudato Si'* affirms,
"The creation accounts in the book of Genesis . . . suggest that human life is grounded in three fundamental
and closely intertwined relationships: with God, with
our neighbor, and with the earth itself. According to the
Bible, these three vital relationships have been broken,
both outwardly and within us. This rupture is sin."[14]

As a spiritual creature, man can only live fearlessly
in free, full connection to the community and its order.
But man has broken the proper communal order that
should reign within himself, between himself and others, himself and God, and all creatures.

The devastation began with a single lie attractively
dangled from the forked tongue of Satan. All sin proceeds from a lie carefully crafted by "the spirit of sin" to
be deceitfully attractive in order to trap. Like fish nib-
bling and nosing the bait, we find that there's enough
truth to tastefully justify a subtle falseness. We consider,
ruminate, and desire before finally swallowing the lie
whole and are all but disemboweled when the reality
inevitably becomes fully apparent.

White Liar

My father is as devastatingly handsome and charismatic as Narcissus. I seem to have known from birth I could easily be sucked into the black hole of his magnetism and disappear completely if I weren't careful. I stood as close to him as I could while retaining the ability to breathe.

Since he was a career military pilot and highway patrolman, our family understood law if nothing else. This was ironic, since I was a criminal responsible for vast networks of lies before the age of ten. I can't remember a sustained period before I was on my own that I did not carry an oppressive, pervasive fear of the atom bomb of my father's detection.

In preschool a boho leather purse with giant sunflowers embroidered on it came home with me and hid under my bed. In kindergarten it was a Peppermint Pattie from the secretary's desk that jumped into my mouth while waiting for a paddling from the principal, and I surely had no idea how the wrapper became lodged in my sock. At nine or so I was shipped with a switch until there were scabby stripes on my legs. When school administrators made inquiries, I was sentenced by my father to wearing pants for the last sweaty months of the year; that seemed to be another "punishment" for my inadequacy.

Every grading period, homework I had nerved over under my father's enforcement would inexplicably disappear between my house and school, but the questions and warning notes of missing assignments and falling grades never made it home or, once I was old enough to craft them convincingly, they trembled under the weight of forged signatures before being handed over.

I changed the Bs on my report cards to As, first with crayon and later with the very pens that awarded them. My dad used booby traps to catch me sneaking into areas of the house that were off-limits, and once I figured them out, I regularly swiped ice-cream money and used his cunning to protect my own secrets from him just to prove I could. A longtime latchkey kid, I learned to field the phone calls that would expose my carefully crafted veneer until the inevitable happened.

I learned to lie from a consummate gaslighter—carefully, convincingly, and often—in order to delay the explosion, but there was always some strange relief mixed into the fear every time it detonated. My father would tell you I have a vivid imagination about things that never happened. For instance, I know or have imagined what it's like to be choked against a wall while dangling a foot or more off the ground.

But after the explosion, silent treatment always followed, and unless I imagined it, that was another backward relief. Once the full extent of my crimes was exposed in the fallout, I spent many moons "on restriction."

Every toy, picture, decoration, and entertainment, including the musical jewelry box with the twirling ballerina—everything but my bed and clothes—was removed from my room. I was allowed to sit, read, or do educational workbooks on my bed. I could use the toilet or eat, but I was forbidden to speak unless spoken to. I became a bomb myself, the ticker winding tighter and tighter the older I got until I hurled my pet hamster against the wall and beat my head on the floorboards in desperation to stop the never-ending agony of being so *bad*.

My behavior was puzzling and disturbing, so I saw a "kid shrink" a few times where I drew pictures—with hands covered in self-inflicted bite marks—of houses happily decorated with flowers, families, and rainbows. The doctor's expert evaluation brought some relief in antidepressants, accelerated classes, and short-lived behavior-modification techniques I cooperated with for the rewards. But none of it stuck; nothing else changed.

So I was like the family dog that pees at the thunder of loud voices, relentlessly licking at my father's hand for the absentminded pat on the head and knowing when to slink out of sight or be kicked there. Until my parents divorced, I continued to act out in ways equivalent to messing on the floor at the most inconvenient moments. By then sneaking and lying were automatic.

That's not to say my problem with lying didn't bother me. I lived in fear of God and constant fear of exposure. But more than even the fear, I was a sensitive soul, and although when I obeyed God I did it out of fear, I knew lying was bad. I knew *I* was bad. If I had been less scared or shrewd, I might have gone to jail before God began turning me around.

The embarrassment came to a head when, completely supporting myself and attending college on scholarship in my late teens, I answered an ordinary question from my dad with an automatic lie. I had a problem, he mocked; I needed mental help; there was something genuinely wrong with me; I was a liar; only a shrink could help me; and he would pay for it.

I was disgusted too for putting myself in a defensive position where he was concerned; I was always on defense with my father, and that was revolting. But I also knew he was right; lies just came frolicking uncontrollably out of my mouth. He found the best psychiatrist at the nearest psych ward in the state, and I went, shoving a magazine cover from the waiting room into the doctor's hand on the first visit with the headline, "The Pathological Liar."

"This is me," were my first words, after which he asked about my relationship with my father, and I collapsed in sobs and tears. I never went back, and I never had to. That was the first and best hundred dollars my dad stuck me with, because I discovered in thirty minutes what my parents learned almost a decade before: that men in authority, especially aggressive ones, triggered my rage and lying. I raged[15] and lied out of fear, I did it automatically, and I did it to escape reality. It was an awful self-fulfilling cycle.

I asked some hard questions: I had my own apartment, worked and went to school full-time. I was for all intents and purposes an adult, even if I couldn't vote yet. Why was I so petrified of my dad? He couldn't actually *do* anything to me anymore except scream at me, and that wasn't really going to *hurt* me. I lied out of a need to feel safe or loved, but that itself was a lie of the tempter meant to keep me enslaved.

The truth was, I didn't have to lie to anyone ever again, and to do so gave away my power, just as Eve had; I became insecure and defensive, and lied more to cover the first lie. Lying was second nature to me, but it was not indicative of the person I wanted to be or that God had created me to be.

I cannot convey how it felt finally to be paroled by a single, honest, trembling syllable: *yes.* I remember the admission as an act of defiance that almost dared my dad to punish me, knowing I could say the words, knowing it was right, and knowing he had no right to the power of fear over me. Aware that a probationary period was prudent until I could form a new habit of honesty, I stepped through the gates of that prison of fear for good and would never turn back to the lie as a way of life.

The Spirit of Truth Is Fearless

Jesus promised, "If you continue in my word, . . . you will know the truth, and the truth will make you free" (Jn 8:31–32). Loyalty to truth makes self-deceit, and therefore deceit from without, impossible. In the Bible, truth is not simply fact; it's *reality*, reality personified and communicated in Christ. Anything less than fidelity to reality is capitulation to Satan, the lie personified and communicated as the "liar and the father of lies" (Jn 8:44), and an open invitation to his wrecking ball of fear and lies.

I continued to struggle with dishonesty and am sometimes still tempted by it when that historical emotion of "being bad" is tweaked and I am desperate not to disappoint someone I respect. But now I know lies are simply the strategy of the enemy to keep me trapped in fear. I remain in constant reconnaissance of my spiritual landscape for breaches in my peace that indicate I may be entertaining a lie. It's a vigilance that keeps me hungry for authenticity, so that truth is emotionally "safe," and I can keep pushing toward deeper reality and transparency.

That hunger for truth turned out to be an ironic gift from the very man who triggered my sin and fear, because it led me straight into the arms of a fearless love where I discovered the reinforcement of community.

Let's Review

- *God created all things in perfect balance*: "God saw everything that he had made, and behold, it was very good" (Gn 1:31).

- *Rebellion is the root of all sin*, chaos, and disorder.

- *Rebellion was the mouth from which Satan lied* to Adam and Eve.

- *In exchanging "the truth about God for a lie,"* our first parents immediately experienced fear (Rom 1:25; see also Gn 3:8–10).

- *Satan "is a liar and the father of lies"* (Jn 8:44). He tempts me with lies in order to separate me from the love of God and others.

- *Lying includes not only false words but also pretense,* deception, or fakeness.

- *All suffering in the world is somehow, mysteriously, the result of sin.*

- Sin causes chaos and disorder; chaos and disorder cause fear; *rebellion and lies cause fear.*

An Invitation

One of the great bits of wisdom in the Genesis account is the insight it provides into Satan's strategies against us. A cursory investigation of my own life reveals he uses the same methods. Spiritual warfare takes place first in the mind; it is won or lost in the battle over temptation to sin, which always begins with a lie. Like everything else, temptation follows a distinct pattern. St. Augustine outlined *three stages in the pattern of sin.*[16] When I know this pattern, I am able to discern its subtlety in action.

Suggestion. Often temptation comes from the devil, but sometimes I just decide to leave God for myself. Either way, the gateway to sin is a simple thought, a suggestion of something attractive, or something I already desire. The enemy doesn't say, "Nobody cares about you. This will help. You'll feel better. You deserve it. You can't help it. They won't know. Who would blame you? This is how you hide it. You've already done it now, so you might as well do it again. It's not that bad anyway."

Instead, he says, "Nobody cares about me. I'm so lonely. It'll make me feel better. I can't help it. I deserve it. At least I'm not as bad as she is. Nobody knows. Might as well go ahead, now. It's not that bad anyway. I'll go to Confession."

Although the story of the Fall is presented to us in third person, notice in your own life that the suggestion always enters the mind as though it comes from inside yourself in order to conceal its deceit. Rather than *You should do this*, we think, *I should do this*.

At this stage, there is no sin. No matter how dangerous the suggestion, it's just a thought, and we have control over our thoughts to make them "obey Christ" (2 Cor 10:5). Thoughts might be insistent and we may almost obsess over them, but remember that temptation only lasts a short while at a time. Notice the lies and half-truths, especially *nobody cares* or *nobody cares about me*. Thoughts are the entry point, the place and time to stand firm, because the Bible says if we ignore or counter the thoughts, they will go away. This is where and when Jesus resisted temptation: immediately. The more we entertain these thoughts, the more insistent they become, until . . .

Pleasure. Instead of ignoring her thoughts, Eve carries on a conversation with the serpent, during which he finds more area to operate. Exorcists say no one should ever "dialogue" with Satan because he is too cunning and will confuse us into submission. Notice how he massages the suggestion, countering Eve's arguments until it is convincing. The flesh is drawn to the suggestion and experiences a certain pleasure in it. For us, this conversation is internal. As yet there is still no sin because the will has not consented, but Eve's willingness to consider and justify assenting to the suggestion is dangerous because it leads to consent.

Consent. Augustine says, "If the will withholds acquiescence, combats the temptation, and repels it, it has scored a success and performed a highly meritorious act. If, on the contrary, the will delights in the pleasure, willingly enjoys it and consents to it, the sin is committed."[17]

After a lengthy conversation, the serpent's suggestion has burrowed into Eve's heart where it has become irresistible and cannot be easily renounced. She wants what is attractive and has ceased resisting what she now desires. She has imagined some "good" she will obtain and has therefore mentally and emotionally possessed it as her own. She could still decide not to eat the fruit, but she no longer wants to. Eve knows she should not do it but chooses to do so anyway. And then she's trapped.

Surrendering to sin weakens the spirit. An attraction to sin develops, which becomes a habit. The habit becomes a stronghold, so powerful that it is almost impossible to face or conquer it. "Every one who commits sin is a slave to sin" (Jn 8:34). "Commits sin" here means having an ongoing habit of sin.

On the other hand, resisting the temptation strengthens the capacity to resist further. This is why we should see temptation as not simply an affliction but a means of permanently overcoming our fears and sin habits.

If left unchecked and unconfessed, sin and evil continue to communicate and cause more harm. No one sins in isolation. Each of us sins against ourselves and every other. Every sin, no matter how small, has consequences attached to it that affect those around us. Relationship is broken. Guilt and fear characterize my life and relationships. We hide from God and each other, running further and further away from forgiveness and intimacy.

If you need to, turn back to the God Prompt from the previous chapter. Now that the scriptures have shed some light on its true destruction, if you're willing, we're going to bring our sin to God and begin working to eliminate it with him.

God Prompt

When God began working with me on my lying problem, he did it just as he did with his Old Testament children: he started with my outward behavior and moved steadily inward to the motivations and wounds behind the behavior. I already knew lying was a sin. The fear and trouble of my sin continually alerted me to that fact through other people. The longer I lied out of fear, the more depressed I became at how *bad* I was and the more anxious I was that I would be found out. Possessing a hideous conceit and low self-esteem in equal measure, I lied to look and seem exceptional, to make myself and others believe I was better than I really was.

As children reacting to overwhelming family dynamics, we develop coping mechanisms to handle emotions, traumas, or family situations that are out of our control. But at some point we become adults in whom the coping mechanism is still unconsciously operating.[18]

Like the Old Testament children of God, all of my religious training to that point had been behavior based, something like, *God is good. You are bad. Stop it.* But that wasn't enough for me to change permanently. Is it enough for you? Have any of your attempts to eliminate sin like this ever worked? You probably have a different sin pattern and root, but the results are the same for all of us. Acting on that sin produces a cycle of anxiety and fear, depression, and more sin.

Thank God for the freedom from sin he gives through Jesus. How about we try something different—something *more* and something deeper? St. Thomas Aquinas once said that since no man can live without joy, one who is deprived of spiritual delight goes over to carnal pleasures.[19] How about we, as Aquinas says, begin finding our delight in God and formulating a strategy to eliminate the sin from our lives?

First, what if our regular examination of conscience becomes more than an attempt to list all we have done wrong during the day or week? Think about the sin issue you brought to God in the last chapter. (From now on we're going to label it "the sorrow," so we're always on the same page.) The sorrow is the sin from chapter 1's God Prompt that you feel God wants you to work with him to eliminate from your life. Take some time in God's presence to review the sorrow in the context of the pattern of sin in the Invitation above. Inviting the Holy Spirit to help you, and in his presence, investigate the progression of lies you personally go through with this sin and how your *thoughts* lead you to *act* on the sorrow.

Can you discern whether your issue with fear, anxiety, or depression has anything to do with the sorrow? Would you say the sorrow is a rare occurrence, a habit, or a stronghold?

"We crush the serpent's head when we extirpate
from our heart the beginnings of temptation," encouraged St. Gregory.[20] The serpent may hiss and threaten,
but he cannot hurt us if we resist him. Spend a few
moments (maybe the week too) meditating on the following verse below. You might want to emphasize each
word or phrase in turn until you have emphasized them
all.

> *"Resist* the devil and he will flee from you" (Jas
> 4:7).
> "Resist *the* devil and he will flee from you"
> (Jas 4:7).
> "Resist the *devil* and he will flee from you"
> (Jas 4:7).

Second, once the devil is on the run, we want to
keep him at bay. Remembering that you're in his presence this very moment, ask the Holy Spirit to help you
formulate a "way of escape" when the temptation to
the sorrow assails you. Maybe you can change your
regular habits to avoid particular places, people, or circumstances of temptation, or share your struggle with
someone for accountability. I have done all of these at
times, and sometimes all at once. Listen for his answer
as you meditate on the following verse: "No temptation
has overtaken you that is not common to man. God is
faithful, and he will not let you be tempted beyond your
strength, but with the temptation will also provide the
way of escape, that you may be able to endure it" (1 Cor
10:13).

Now that we have acknowledged the enemy and
unveiled his strategy, I pray you will spend as much
time as necessary knowing yourself and knowing your
enemy, and formulating your "way of escape." I pray

you will throw yourself completely on God's mercy as you attempt to combat this temptation in his presence and with his help every moment. Make no compromise! Third, a significant part of any spiritual strategy must be the sacraments. What might happen if you make the sorrow a matter of weekly Confession and receive the Eucharist with the intention of fortifying you from the sorrow? What if you also confided and "confessed" to a spouse, relative, or friend for accountability?

Other helps include the following: Keep your list of scriptures handy, and say them aloud or under your breath in moments of temptation, realizing it will not last long. Make a gratitude list. Careful, deliberate thankfulness for our blessings often mitigates the desire to sin.

Another "way of escape" that helps me is a suggestion Leah Libresco made in *Arriving at Amen*. When you're in a moment of temptation, praying a single Hail Mary allows just a few moments of separation between the suggestion and pleasure parts of the sin pattern and helps break its almost hypnotic power. If you're having trouble with falling to the sorrow before you've even recognized you're being tempted, ask your guardian angel to bring it clearly to mind *before* you fall, so you can be more conscious.

Above all, "let us not grow weary in well-doing, for in due season we shall reap, if we do not lose heart" (Gal 6:9). God does not grow weary or lose patience with us no matter how frequently we succumb to the sorrow. Think about it: he already knows exactly how many failed attempts are required to conquer it, and every attempt gets us one closer than we were before to the final number when we are free! Never give up, Dear One. Never, never, never give up.

3

*F*earless Reinforcement

Returning to Community

The holiday season is supposed to be a time of cheer and relaxation, the "most wonderful time of the year," as the song says. But I know from experience that the reputation for family eruptions that the holidays have also acquired is well earned. This past holiday season was an unmatched gauntlet for head-exploding drama and heart-pounding anxiety on both sides of our family. An eerily similar craziness boiled over from two different, unrelated people in two different, unrelated occasions separated by several weeks.

I'm no prophet, but I have learned through discerning my patterns that,[1] when I see or hear something two or more times, I can be sure God is at work somehow. I know to pay attention to what happens next and be in prayer about the people and circumstances around me, because they are being used by the Holy Spirit to teach me something (Jn 5:19). So the theatrics flanking the season sent warning bells ringing in my head as soon as the second emotional tornado hit. Baseless accusations, foaming rage, vociferous cursing, unjustifiable suspicion, and alternative realities left us all reeling in confusion during the season of "heavenly peace." *Do you hear what I hear? What in the world is happening? Is it us? Is it them?*

Having shared the lovely experience of living for years with a consummate gaslighter, you would think we'd all have pinpointed the strategy immediately, but apparently a twenty-five-year separation from direct, daily exposure makes one rusty. I felt foolish that it took me so long to discern that volatile relationship dynamics my family has struggled with for years are the result of a relative's latent personality disorder. I was thankful and relieved to have answers to recent, desperate prayers for guidance on how to deal with the tangled issues surrounding the important relationship, but the answers have been difficult to accept. Tragically, unfortunate family patterns of emotional abuse are being perpetuated, as former victims have become perpetrators themselves.

I walked away from the Tasmanian devil with a heavy spirit and desperate prayers for peace, because I know her pain. I was a devil myself for similar reasons. As sympathetic and open hearted as I am, as much as I love and want to be in relationship with her, I know this drill from years of therapy: she is incapable of normal relationships, a damsel who loves her distress. Stewing in a cauldron of pain and anger, such people vomit and project a distorted self-image onto every living thing within a mile radius, and some are only "safe" to love from a distance, emotional or otherwise.

The Hot Mess We're In

Living with the chaos and anxiety of habitual sin, our own or another's, is depressing. We just want *away* from it. Sometimes the consequences of sin, our own or someone else's, linger long after the original circumstances. Flight-or-fight stressors can become so frequent they cause chemical imbalances—physical ruts—that must be medically addressed along with the emotional and spiritual triggers.

Out-of-control weight, relationships, debt, addiction, schedules, children, and disease all combine in enormous, knotted, defeating messes from which we seem unable to extricate ourselves. We need reinforcement. True, it's in relationships that we wound and are wounded, but it's also through relationships that we are redeemed. We must return to the unity of community.

Eden teaches us that God designed us in a state of perpetual need for community. Neediness is not a result of fallenness but createdness. To need one another, to need help, to need guidance, and to need God is not because Adam and Eve did anything wrong. Their neediness was not sin; it was ultimate perfection. Their relationship with God and one another was perfectly designed so that they could easily recognize their needs and transcend them by resisting self-sufficiency and depending on God to provide for them.

But sin divides and isolates us; it separates us in fear from one another, from God, and from ourselves. Because the circular relationship is secondarily physical, all other temporal affiliations are also affected. All of creation was desecrated by the power grab. We no longer go to God with our needs. Others are not always a soft or even safe place for us.

Sometimes people have to separate themselves from us for their protection; sometimes we have to separate ourselves from them for the same reason. And yet, "O happy fault that earned for us so great, so glorious a redeemer"; sin's grasp is not the last word.[2]

Can you believe it? Right now, an even higher, *more* perfect state than Eden is possible *despite* sin. That means the painful chaos in my life, even when it's of my own making, can be reordered in a way that is even better than it would have been had I or someone else not made such an awful mess of things.

How does God reorder? He begins higher than nature, higher than our pains and messes, and reaches down in grace with Trinitarian community.

Grace Is a Fat Lady

The simplest, most practical, active definition of grace I know is to treat someone better than she or he deserves. God treats us better than we deserve by refusing to abandon us to the painful tragedies of sin. Most people start with the agony of sin and wonder why. Why is there cancer, rape, abuse, war, hunger, murder, poverty, and disease? *Why does such terrifying, endless suffering exist?* is one of the most frequent questions people ask about faith and God. Instead, I would counter, *In the face of all the injustices and indignities I personally inflict against him, myself, and other people, why does God treat me with grace?*

Try multiplying your own sins of a single day by the number of days in your lifetime, and those of the lifetimes of the number of people who exist, and have ever existed, or will exist, and all their degrees of sin and evil compounded throughout the history of mankind. What is so astounding about suffering, to me, then, is not *that* we suffer. Suffering seems natural and obvious once one understands something of the catastrophe incurred by our parents' choice to leave the circle of relationship that protected us all. Furthermore, in my own day-to-day life, how would I learn to choose more wisely if there were not consequences for sin?

No, what shocks me more than the reality of suffering is the *power of love*, the ability—and yes, the *willingness*—of God to reenter the scenario, to reconcile everything under the slavery and fear of sin, and reorder all that suffering to himself through millennia upon millennia of souls and sins and years. The angels chose to rebel, and God left them in their fallen state forever. Why not man?

In the car, on the way home from the head-exploding drama with that family member, I asked the Lord, "Why do you even *bother* with us? How can you expect me to bother with *her*?" Truly, only divine love could bother; it is a higher love in the supernatural order of grace. And how *powerful* one "drop" of that love must be if goodness and love not only exist, but thrive and conquer the oceans and eons of sin and misery.

Even while pointing out the truth of the profound, enduring consequences of that first sin to the first sinners, the Giver planted the seeds and prophecy of returning to him through the woman (Gn 3:15). God would do with the hot mess of mankind what mankind could never do for itself: he would make it possible to return to the circle of relationship established in Eden, but in a way that communicates God's matchless power even more beautifully, through the rush of grace leaping from the heart of the Giver into the hemorrhaging wound of sin. "Where sin increased, grace abounded all the more" (Rom 5:20).

Wouldn't only an impotent God allow a malicious, jealous angel the last word regarding all he fashioned and loved? As they say, "It ain't over till the fat lady sings." Grace is the fat lady in the opera of suffering, in full-throated vibrato. As Flannery O'Connor expressed, the central Christian mystery is such that life, "for all its horror, has been found by God to be worth dying for."[3] If our horror has been found by God to be worth dying for, there is sure to be purpose and meaning in it. Could our return to community somehow be related to *my* relationship to suffering? And could it have something, especially, to do with my own womanhood?

The Great Rewind

As C. S. Lewis wrote in *The Great Divorce*, "A sum can be put right: but only by going back till you find the error and working it afresh from that point, never by simply going on. Evil can be undone, but it cannot 'develop' into good. Time does not heal it. The spell must be unwound, bit by bit, 'with backward mutters of dissevering power'—or else not."[4]

Approaching Eve first seems to have been a deliberate strategy, as though Satan knew or suspected that she was somehow foundational to it all and to convince her would be the key to destroying the whole structure. That, to me, along with Eve's resultant dispossession of authority and subjection to Adam, suggests that Eve both enjoyed and abused some sort of profound influence prior to the Fall. Whatever it means, God used the same woman-first approach when the "fullness of time had come" (Gal 4:4, NABRE). As St. John Paul II reminded us, "God entrusted the human being to woman. Certainly, every human being is entrusted to each and every other human being, but in a special way the human being is entrusted to woman, precisely because the woman in virtue of her special experience of motherhood is seen to have a specific sensitivity towards the human person and all that constitutes the individual's true welfare."[5]

Woman it was through whom the ancient wound first entered, and woman it would be through whom the Great Return would begin. God began redemption by rewinding to the beginning, the woman, where the sin first rooted, burrowed, and poisoned. All of time works backward from Mary's "yes."

In the cosmic battle between good and evil, woman is said to be the companion and helpmate to man. She is a "helper" or battle partner "suitable" or "fit" for him, meaning his opposite or complement (Gn 2:18).

Elsewhere this designation is used for the Holy Spirit himself (see Jn 14:16–17). The actual term used is *Paraclete*, itself a battle word that conveys the idea of coming alongside to surround, advise, guard, protect, and aid.

Edith Stein, a saintly Catholic feminist and profound philosopher gassed at Auschwitz, observed, "The terms 'woman' and 'offspring' [in the proto-evangelium] designate the Mother of God and the Redeemer. This, however, does not exclude the other meaning; the first woman, to whom Adam gave the name 'mother of all living creatures,' as well as all her successors had been given a particular duty to struggle against evil and to prepare for the spiritual restoration of life."[6]

The distinction of the female sex is that woman was the first to be tempted and the first to hear the message of God's grace, "and each time woman's assent determined the destiny of humanity as a whole."[7]

The spiritual restoration of life began with the willingness of one woman to completely obey and follow God in the context of her regular duties and station. What if that's also true of each woman and the realm commended to her?

If woman *is* specially charged with the battle against evil in her professional and domestic realms, might each woman's assent also mysteriously restore life in those entrusted to her?

The redemption of your terrifying hot mess begins with you. You too must reenter community in the same way you left it: returning to God, returning to self, and returning to others.

Like Mary, I can receive the Word of God in truth and return all that pertains to me to his provision. In returning, I reclaim my rightful dignity and mysterious influence as woman, fearless and immovable. In reclaiming my dignity, I am able to safely reenter relationships, accepting in his grace all those around me with their faults intact; and in reentering, I reproduce the Word in the world.

Returning Looks Like This

In our twenty-three years of marriage my husband and I have had only two ongoing fighting issues: his critical spirit versus my "oversensitivity," and his unwillingness to carry a balance or even use our one credit card versus my willingness to carry a small (never more than three thousand dollars) balance and my need to use it for travel and ministry.

Every time I used the card he would get mad, even if it was, in my mind, absolutely necessary. I was checked out at the grocery store with small children and a full cart when I discovered I had accidently left my debit card at home. I paid with the credit card to keep from holding up the line but was informed I should have left the groceries in the store and gone to the bank, with the kids, past lunchtime and near naptime, to get cash and check out all over again rather than use the credit card. I kid you not. (Does anyone else find this absurdly *absurd*? I am getting angry just writing about it!)

We have always agreed on only ever having one card, so I began either telling him I had bought something ahead of the statement or putting the cash aside to cover my purchases, because it seemed to be the surprise on the statements that irritated him. Well, that didn't completely alleviate the conflict either, and we've had several doozy fights over this issue. He just didn't want any balance on the card, ever.

I have many other glaring faults, but I am not and never have been motivated by money; we have very little debt, and I don't buy much (we're both this way, actually), so I found his zero-use policy completely unreasonable. I am, after all, a grown, frugal, intelligent woman, able to make my own decisions and pay my own way without any need whatsoever of consulting him.

I never stopped using it, and I finally told him in as haughty a voice as I could muster that I never would, but we were not going to fight over it ever again. Ever. Again. Because I was sick of his attempts to force and control (power grab) and would buy whatever I needed or wanted within reason whenever I needed or wanted it without necessarily consulting him (the retaliatory power grab), and he could puff up like a bullfrog all he wanted. He stopped huffing and puffing over it just so I wouldn't carry through with my threat, and there was a stalemate. But then I had a most enlightening conversation with a friend.

A fellow book lover and homeschooler, she had gotten an Amazon rewards card with which she paid every household bill and expense so she could rack up thousands of points a month to use toward free books. UPS was at her house almost every day of every week. When I saw how she was working the system for all those books, my eyes bugged out like Roger Rabbit clapping eyes on Jessica for the first time. I could smell the new pages of all the books I would get and feel their crispiness in my hands.

The Lord had taught me the circular relationship principle, and I practiced it without too much difficulty throughout our marriage because my husband is reasonable about most things and we are usually unreasonable together on whatever is left. But I knew this would never fly, so I applied for the credit card without telling him and used it secretly for three months. I had the statements delivered and paid the payments electronically. I used it for groceries, gas, and airline tickets. I was rolling in free books! And about a month in, just as I was basking in my wisdom, the Lord began bringing it up in daily prayer: "Wives, be subject to your husbands, as to the Lord" (Eph 5:22). Oh, boy.

Why had I not trusted him with the outcome of talking to my husband about the card, when I had done so with everything else? Did I not think God could provide whatever I needed and a lot of what I wanted without my being deceitful? Hadn't he had a free antique piano delivered to my door that time I tentatively asked him for one? And then there was the exorbitantly expensive stained-glass church window I couldn't afford and begged him for years ago; hadn't he surprised me with *two* of them several months later?

When I asked him to wake me up at a certain time of morning, had he ever let me oversleep? How many times have I gone to him melancholy or lonely when, without fail, he sent an unexpected card, surprise phone call, or tender hug from wiry, little-boy arms? Had he not proven over and over that all I needed to do was ask him and he would do *something* if I would wait on him? I was cut to the heart.

So I pitched the card idea to my husband, systematically laying out the whys as if it were a high-stakes business negotiation. He said no. I waited a week and then made *sure* he knew how important it was to me and how practical for homeschool curriculum expenses. He said no. I asked a week later, whining a little and getting angry, but he wouldn't budge. I was stuck in the guilt of deceit and rebellion against my husband.

Or, to put it more acceptably since letting one's husband dictate her behavior is said to be unacceptably weak, I was stuck in "rebellion" against him. Here's where the rubber meets the road, ladies: I have heard many Eves say they must wear the pants in their family because the husband won't, but may I suggest necessity is rarely the issue? Isn't the truth, rather, that we won't wait and keep our hands off the circumstance long enough for God to handle it through our husbands, and when he does, we don't usually like how he does it? Aren't we afraid to trust God through a decision we wouldn't have made, a financial difficulty, a parenting fail, or any other inconvenient thing he might let our husbands "get us into"?

Jesus challenges that approach: "Give, and it will be given to you; good measure, pressed down, shaken together, running over, will be put into your lap. For the measure you give will be the measure you get back" (Lk 6:38). By jumping in to "handle" things, we give nothing to God; we risk next to nothing in trusting him and then complain that we get next to nothing from him or our husbands.

I'm not blowing sparkles and bubbles in your face. I understand terrible husbands, but Jesus is not one of them. Unless there's sin involved, why not try asking God for what you need, back off completely (totally), and wait as long as it takes to see what he does? And if that prospect is simply untenable, can we at least admit it's so and stop pretending we're following God in this area?

I wonder how long Mary waited on God to send Joseph the dream that confirmed her purity? Was it hard for her to refrain from defending herself in the community while praying that God would do it for her? While waiting for him to decide, did she pack up the baby and the house and tell Joseph it was time to go to Egypt while mounting the donkey and "letting" him walk? Did she complain when he took her to a barn to give birth to the Savior of the world?

Is it because Mary is so submissive to God that she is so powerful?

Because my entire spiritual education has been based on learning a proper understanding of authority, I get this pop quiz on a regular basis. I know it's not really my husband to whom I "submit" but God himself.[8] And that makes it easier, truly. Obviously I don't practice this "submission" as well as I know I can and should; I knew getting that card in the first place was stepping outside community in deceit; that's why I hid it. And keeping it after my husband expressed serious misgivings was being disobedient to God's "no" and remaining there.

Repent, Return, Reenter, Re-late

I knew there had to be a good reason for God to say no through my husband even though I couldn't see one through all the "advantages" of having it. I knew if my husband found out, he would be angry and hurt. I finally *repented* (meaning to change direction), *returned* to God's provision, and *reentered* the circle of *relationship* with both God and my husband; I cut up the card under the excruciation of saying goodbye to all those free books. Almost immediately afterward, I experienced a monumental spiritual breakthrough in my life, but the inevitable consequences of my sin had yet to be felt (Wis 11:16; Rom 6:23).

I did not tell my husband about any of it even after I had cut up the card. Instead, he found out when an "errant" paper statement arrived before I could formally close the account. I was so proud that I had cut it up, but he understandably felt deeply betrayed by my deceit because I had never done something secretly like that before, and our relationship was painfully strained for weeks. See how grasping outside my relationship with God and my husband was a move for personal power that disconnected me to some degree from both of them?

That I should have something God did not want me to have and that I could take it for myself rather than receiving it from him without incurring consequences was a lie meant to separate me from myself, from God, and from my husband. And it worked. Attracted by the promise of loads of books, I made the power grab and stepped out from under God's provision and protection, caused a division in my marriage, and felt the fear and guilt of being found out.

Only because I fully repented and reentered the relationship circle by both asking for forgiveness *and* cutting up the credit card was I willing and able simply to experience my husband's disappointed, angry reaction, and even the reality of my own sin without judgment. Trust and intimacy with God and with my husband was reestablished. And because the guilt was removed from my conscience and out in the open, I was "returned" to myself. I had returned fully to the community that protects, provides for, and reinforces me.

That beautiful section in Ephesians about sacramental marriage as the mysterious reflection of Christ's relationship to the Church begins, "Be subject to one another out of reverence for Christ" (Eph 5:21). The Church submits to Christ because he sacrifices everything for her. You may say your husband does not sacrifice everything for you, but do you defer to his wishes? Someone has to suffer humility first to begin renewal. God suffered in humility for our renewal in Christ. Mary, full of grace, suffered humility for our renewal. What if that's what grace, particularly marital grace, is for?

Every woman likes to think, *Of course I care about having a better relationship. Of course I want a strong influence. Of course I want to be closer to God.* But most of the time we only submit to others if they deserve it or if we're going to gain from it ourselves somehow. When we survey the tangled, contentious messes and gaping deficiencies in our relationships and the sin in our lives, we don't think first, for example, *Let me surrender what I want so he can have what he wants.* We don't hurry to ask ourselves, *How can I be crazy generous in this confrontation, in this day, and in this moment?* What springs to mind first is rarely *How can I receive this person, faults and all?* or *Does God want me to have this?*

Instead, we think, *I'd love to be less selfish, but he doesn't appreciate me.* Or *I want to experience renewal in my relationship, but he has to apologize first.* We prevaricate and deflect behind *You go first. You say you're sorry, and I might forgive you. You change, and I might change. You be transparent, and then I'll be transparent. You quit fighting, and then I'll quit fighting.*[9]

But "God entrusted the human being to woman" because she has a specific sensitivity to the human person's true welfare. I am woman; renewal begins with me. I must repent of my gracelessness, return everything involved to God's provision, reenter the communion of God's embrace, and re-relate to others in and with the supernatural grace that flows from that reinforcement. In doing so I am open and able to receive those around me, flaws and all.

I am woman. I must go first.

Once, When We Did It Right...

When I began making my way into full communion with the Church, friends of mine quoted Ephesians 5:22 to me, "Wives be subject to your husbands," and either implied or actually stated that I was being disobedient to God simply because I knew my husband didn't like my conversion and I was doing it anyway.

Because I have spent many years learning about a proper relationship to authority, I struggled with this accusation a lot. Either I was being disobedient to God by doing something my husband did not agree with (did I just see you roll your eyes?), or I was being disobedient to God by not following the truth to the Church: "Whoever knows what is right to do and fails to do it, for him it is sin" (Jas 4:17).

As hard as it was on my husband for me to go off on a religious tangent (in his mind), he never told me not to or that I couldn't, and God protected me from that because I trusted him with the entire process and whatever consequences that might follow obeying him. My husband submitted to my full communion, and it was a painful sacrifice for him. I submitted to his anger, fear, and struggle with all I was doing and tried to make it as easy for him as possible.

Genuine relationships are marked by mutual submission even when the choices seem or are not helpful or healthy. They're not guided by "superiority," slavery, or fear, but love and respect. And only the supernatural grace of God can make them so.

Because I can buy all the books and anything else I want with my debit card or our current credit card, the only reason not to accommodate my husband on the issue of the illicit credit card was because I had a "right" to it and wanted my way. But "rights" are where survivors go so they won't have to work out relationships. In reality, we have no rights as Christians except to submit to one another (Rom 13:10). But as long as we think we do, we will surely become ticked off when someone tells us no, even if it's God.

In the circular relationship that nurtures me, all life, all community, and expectancy, independence must die, because independence fosters fear and isolation against love, force and duty against freedom, and presumption against expectancy. Why?

Grasping for control and independence rather than submitting to God's Providence is resistance to the reality that we are not independent and not in control at all, and this rebellion is sin. Sin causes chaos and disorder. Depression is caused by our living in the disorder of the past. Anxiety is caused by our living in the disorder of the future. Peace comes from dependence on God, because I Am is always in the present moment. If you're overwhelmed by life, return to the immediate present moment and use your five senses to savor all that is beautiful and comforting. Take a deep breath; relax into God.

Give him your worries. The constant anticipation of what he will do and send next, and knowing it all comes from him, relieves the fear and anxiety of difficulties. We are free to love and yield to others in every situation it's needed. His will is done in me as it is in heaven.

Dear One, it is truly Good News that your contemporary Western life will take on the throbbing pulse of heaven when, like the planets and their moons anchored and orbiting around the sun, everything in you and in your life begins to revolve around the Source of community in an inclusive, dependent structure as much as is possible and reasonable: God and you, you and others. Because of Christ's matchless submission to God through us, our own lives can reclaim something better than Eden when this interrelated design and order, this relationship, has been renewed.

Beloved, the Source is inexhaustible. The deeper the abyss of need, the more of God you get. The Giver is all you need. When you stay connected to him and receive from him, you lean into love and away from fear. In the beginning was God, and God created the heavens and the earth. Nothing existed before he made it, and everything created proceeded from him. Isn't providing for it, administrating it, and managing all of it a moral imperative, then? If everything originated with God, shouldn't God provide and care for its every need? Wouldn't anything less be unjust?

In touching, infinite generosity, he has bound himself in unfathomable love and humble service to all he's made, including you and all that concerns you (Ps 138:8).

From Possessing to Praise: The Process

Taking, snatching, grasping, forcing, clutching, and hoarding only ever produce the unrest, disorder, chaos, and fear of knowing and experiencing evil. Dear One, stop trying to earn, take, and hoard what is gift.

That God is the source and giver of everything is a primary point of our faith, but we seldom consider that includes all the stuff of life—education, purpose, meaning, love, knowledge, intimacy, fearlessness, wisdom, peace, and grace—not just matter. When we think of Adam and Eve living "fearless" in Paradise, we should consider God as the giver of their intellectual, physical, emotional, and spiritual Eden. Remember, it's all one life, and in the Garden it was all heaven on earth, perfect abundant life! And all was grace-gift.

What did they need that God did not provide? They lived in radical bliss because God furnished them a comfortable place to live, a comparable mate, intimate relationships, activity that fit their personalities and temperaments, lots to occupy their interests, food and nourishment, and the deep confidence and joy of an uninterrupted communion of grace. Are such things needs or desires? Do you lack any of these? When life is lived according to God's design, he will provide everything I truly need. And once we fully return to community, we begin to experience the wonder of God's matchless, hilarious, almost wasteful generosity.

Hilarious Givers

My favorite pastor of all time, the pastor of the non-Catholic church we were members of prior to my full communion, is an extravagant, hilarious giver. I remember his daughters laughing about how they loved shopping with him because he bought them everything they liked. But what I remember about his generosity is how he dared us all to try to "outgive" God.

I did try: I gave away stuff I loved; I performed random services for strangers; I overtithed on my gross pay; I sacrificed for my husband till it hurt; and I went out of my way in the face of rudeness to do crazy sweet things. I became a "cheerful giver" (*cheerful* is from the same root as *hilarious*), and I discovered that "he who sows sparingly will also reap sparingly, and he who sows bountifully will also reap bountifully. . . . For God loves a cheerful giver. And God is able to provide you with every blessing in abundance, so that you may *always have enough of everything* and may provide in abundance for every good work" (2 Cor 9:6–8, emphasis added).

What a promise! In Paradise, God was the source for all they needed, and they didn't have to do a single thing to receive any of it from him except stay connected to the sap of his grace. Jesus promised, "I am the vine, you are the branches. He who abides in me, and I in him, he it is that bears much fruit, for apart from me you can do nothing. If a man does not abide in me, he is cast forth as a branch and withers; and the branches are gathered, thrown into the fire and burned. If you abide in me, and my words abide in you, ask whatever you will, and it shall be done for you" (Jn 15:5–7). Trust him; he will not "use" you. You can never give too much in God's economy. I dare you to try it.

The risk and sacrifice of submission to God and to others is the key to reentering the life-giving relationship circle that connects us to God and them; that's what community means. Mary shows us that a woman who does it well reflects the rightful dignity of a true and powerful feminine mystique that carries great spiritual weight.

Let's Review

- *Sin disrupts the balance and order God intends for me*, introducing disorder and chaos, and the fear, anxiety, and depression that go with them.

- *God's grace can make my mess better than it would have been if sin had never been involved.*

- *Neediness is part of my createdness* and does not necessarily indicate the presence of a problem or sin.

- *Reentering a dependent relationship that receives from, releases to, and remains in God begins the renewal* of all that has become disordered and fearful in my life.

- *Resting in a dependent relationship begins with submitting to God* through others and trusting him to provide for my needs.

- *Depression is fear from the past. Anxiety is fear of the future. Peace comes from dependence on God in the present.*

An Invitation

I mentioned earlier that one of the two ongoing issues in our twenty-three-year marriage has been my husband's critical spirit and my "oversensitivity" to criticism. I put that in quotes because it annoys me so much, but my condemning childhood left me with a hypersensitivity

to criticism, and my husband has always been an Eey-
ore for whom most things will surely come to the worst
possible conclusion and the glasses of life are always
half empty and leaking.

As a result of a lifetime of dealing with critical pessi-
mism, I can talk myself off just about any ledge and persevere in the trenches long after most people have given
up or died, as long as I pray through it, but sometimes
his negativity just sucks the life out of me. I remember
sobbing over my hurt feelings to a mentor once, telling
her I felt nothing I did ever pleased him, that he had so
little to say that was supportive or complimentary, and
how disgusting it was to me that I was so needy. She told
me to talk to Jesus about it and tell him what I wanted
and needed. I said, "I feel like such a baby going to the
Lord about such dumb, little, immature things!"

The Lord sent her next sentence rolling into my soul
and echoing there like a great thunderclap: "You *are* his
baby."

You are his baby, Dear One.

God Prompt

*What was the most significant sentence, scripture, passage,
or idea you read in this chapter?* Was there any place that
caused a strong reaction of some kind—perhaps longing,
perhaps anxiety, or perhaps a flash of insight? If anything particularly struck you in this chapter, how is it the
voice of God, acting and moving in your heart and life?

How can re-penting, re-turning, re-entering, and
re-lating help you overcome the sorrow? How can
receiving from, releasing to, and remaining in God begin
the renewal of all that has become disordered and fearful
in your life through the sorrow?

Probe for the temptation. When are you tempted to "go it alone," to provide for yourself without thought, petition, or waiting on God as your provider? In your relationship with God, where are you tempted to presumptuousness, or to assert authority when it is not rightfully yours? In your relationship with others, when are you tempted to criticize and make judgments that you are not qualified to make?

Probe for the lie. How does a disruption of relationship in one of these areas lead to distance and disorder in others rather than getting you the result you want? Has there ever been a time when you needed the kind of help you could not get directly from God? Is there ever such a time?

Try to hear him speak through the Word. Remembering that you are his baby, spend some time meditating on the following verse in his presence. You may want to emphasize each word in turn like this:

> "*And* my God will supply every need of yours according to his riches in glory in Christ Jesus" (Phil 4:19).
>
> "And *my* God will supply every need of yours according to his riches in glory in Christ Jesus" (Phil 4:19).
>
> "And my *God* will supply every need of yours according to his riches in glory in Christ Jesus" (Phil 4:19).
>
> "And my God *will* supply every need of yours according to his riches in glory in Christ Jesus" (Phil 4:19).

Part of what I love about this verse is the reminder that if I don't have it after asking and waiting for him, I don't need it. When I have turned to God to meet my needs, whatever they are, he has always been faithful to provide. Through my mentor's sweet assurance that I am God's baby, I can clamor like a child for his help and rest in his provision. That provision always includes my relationship needs and often even stuff I just want. When I fall into fear, isn't it because I am looking to myself, not to God, for the solution?

But what about those I love? When have you been terrified for the physical or spiritual safety of a child, spouse, or other loved one? "Can any of you by worrying add a single moment to your [or their] life-span?" (Mt 6:27, NABRE). God's love is an intense focus on us and concern for our problems, but never worry. God is never worried. When we are abiding in the one who does not worry, we do not worry either.

Anxiety is an abiding, paralyzing fear about a perceived future and its imagined threats. Ask yourself, *How often does what I obsess over come to pass?* God keeps the future hidden for me, not from me. Ultimately every promise and every answer is in him; he is my "yes" (2 Cor 1:20).

What about when anxiety for the safety of those I love and serve is justified, even if admittedly overblown? What then? What helps me most when I panic or worry about my children and family is remembering they are not my possessions; they are not mine at all. I must detach from the lie that they are mine and release them to the embrace of God, however he chooses to hold them. I am here to hold their hands along the path to sanctity for as long as we have together, and that's a length of time I cannot know. I know that sounds counterintuitive, but it really helps to remember he loves and protects them better than I could.

Remember to go to Confession and receive the Eucharist for the issues you are discovering throughout your study. The sacraments help strengthen us in charity and humility for the battle over our souls and families.

Reinforcement in community is the only way we can not only survive but also thrive, and it's why the enemy's strategy is to divide and conquer us through sin. Returning to communion with God and reaching out to others in community means change, and change means risk. Risk big. As the late Mother Angelica, foundress of EWTN, reportedly quipped, "Unless you are willing to do the ridiculous, God will not do the miraculous."[10]

4

$\mathcal{F}$earless Dignity

Confronting the Feint

My youngest son is a first-year Latin student, and just a few weeks ago I assisted him with a lesson in conjugating the verb *sum*, meaning *to be*. This verb explains how we are, not how we do things; *to be* shows existence, not action. Did you know the verb *to be* is the most common verb in every language? Imagine my glee at the segue this primary Latin lesson offered into a biblical discussion of the otherness of God and the profound dignity of humanity.

But what really shocked me, reflecting further on *to be*, was stumbling upon a perfect outline of the enemy's most pervasive, successful after-sin feint against humankind inherent in the names of things.

The *What* That's in a Name

Rather than a simple moniker or title, names in the scriptures are important. Ancient names were supposed to bear significance, so people's names expressed particular characteristics they possessed: Moses, meaning *drawn out*, as in drawn out of the Nile River and later Egypt; Jacob, meaning *cheater*; and Jesus, meaning *God with us*. Names were carefully and solemnly selected, especially personal names, because they explained, in part, what a thing *was*.

Researching biblical names often supplies information that would otherwise be missed by a simple reading of the text, so I look up almost every biblical name in a concordance. So intimate was the relationship between individuals and their names that "to be called" something meant "to be" that something. Knowing one's name meant knowing the person behind the name. Likewise, to withhold one's name was to withhold the particular intimacy of the "is-ness" of a person.

It Is Too Wonderful

That biblical names tell us what something *is* sheds light on some of my favorite Old Testament adventures involving mysterious "angels of the Lord." They appear to God's people for particular purposes; they speak strangely and do odd, fantastic things.

One such "angel of the Lord" appears to Manoah and his wife to announce that she will conceive and bear a son, Samson, who will one day deliver the Israelites from the oppression of their archrivals, the Philistines. Manoah thinks the angel is just some guy, so he offers to feed him and asks his name: "'What is your name, so that, when your words come true, we may honor you?' And the angel of the Lord said to him, 'Why do you ask my name, seeing it is *wonderful*?'" (Jgs 13:17–18, emphasis added).

The angel's name is too wonderful to reveal, so some translations use the word *secret*—too wonderful, "wondermous."

As though uttering the name might burst an eardrum.

Can the smell of rain be *too* wet? Are a baby's toes too fat? Is spring too fresh, ice cream too cold, or grace too amazing? What name could be so *wonderful* that it must be secret?

In the end, the angel declines the hospitality of their meal, and his name remains a mystery. He "does wondrous things" by causing fire to leap up from the altar rock and consume the sacrifice Manoah offers to God, and then he ascends with it. But the angel is unwilling to reveal his essential character to the couple, embodied in the name, and he never answers their question. Contrast his preference to remain distant with God's intimate, revealing response to Moses's same question.

To Be, or Not to Be, That Is the Question

Moses stands on holy ground; he hides his face, afraid to look on the God calling him from the bush to deliver his people from slavery in Egypt through his miraculous leadership and power (Ex 3:1–6). In the face of the extraordinary presence and voice from inside the flaming but intact bush, somehow Moses has the presence of mind to ask God his name. Was he was trying to pin him down, possibly harkening back to the polytheism of Egypt, looking to identify him with some familiar god?

Whatever it was, anticipating their skepticism, "Moses said to God, 'If I come to the sons of Israel and say to them, "The God of your fathers has sent me to you," and they ask me, "What is his name?" what shall

I say to them?' God said to Moses, 'I am who I am.' And he said, 'Say this to the people of Israel, "I am has sent me to you"'" (Ex 3:13–14).

If the angel of the Lord's name was too wonderful, how must this divine, disembodied name have leaped from the bush like electricity from a high-voltage wire and erupted in a burst of crackling light? The people of Israel had previously distinguished God only as the friend of Abraham, Isaac, and Jacob. Now they and the whole human race know his name. Part of God's promise of deliverance is the assurance he would "be with" his people (Ex 3:12), and now he tells Moses his name is "I am." This self-designation of God is from the verb *to be* and originates from the root *to breathe*. It means, "I exist, I breathe, I live, I am being itself, I am." God is not only his own essence but also his own existence.[1] Self-existent, uncaused, independent, self-identified, and self-sufficient, God was *secret* to humankind until he made himself known.

Conjugating the Latin verb *sum*, that most prolific verb in every language, *to be*—was, is, will be; I am, you are, he is, she is, it is; we are, you all are, they are—I gawked with my little boy at the polyglot realization that all that exists, all that was, is, and will be, proceeds from He is.

Unlike the angel of the Lord who withheld the intimacy of an identifier, God himself stooped down to peer into his friend Moses's face, to personally and tenderly reveal himself in profound simplicity to all humanity as an invitation to an all-consuming intimacy: I am who am. Conveying the scope of this telling is like trying to cram the whole universe into a kangaroo pouch. By saying next to nothing, the name says everything that is, and so exquisitely, as though he had nothing better in all of eternity to do than tell us his secret.

Who *is*? He *is*. And although *to be* is the most common verb in every language, he's the only one who truly *is*. A traditional Jewish understanding of holiness helps explain what I mean.

Holy Terror

Typically, when we think of holiness we think of cleanliness or purity. The word *holy* literally means *other, set apart, sanctified,* and *consecrated*. In the Old Testament, things and people were *set apart* exclusively for God, for the worship of God or for God himself to work, speak, and rule through. To preserve this unique *otherness*, sacred things and people were not to be "used" or even touched in ordinary ways.

The ancient Jews used repetition to express the superlative of holiness. For instance, we say holy, holier, holiest; they said, "Holy, holy, holy is the Lord God Almighty" (Rv 4:8).

To the Jewish mind, this otherness and holiness means more along the lines of *transparency*. God is holy because he is who he is and nothing else. He says of himself, "For I the Lord do not change" (Mal 3:6). Elsewhere, scripture says that in him "there is no variation or shadow due to change" (Jas 1:17).

In the Bible, glimpsing this otherness is felt as fear:

> On the morning of the third day there was thunder and lightning, and a thick cloud upon the mountain, and a very loud trumpet blast, so that all the people who were in the camp trembled. Then Moses brought the people out of the camp to meet God; and they took their stand at the foot of the mountain. And Mount Sinai was wrapped

in smoke, because the Lord descended upon it in
fire; and the smoke of it went up like the smoke
of a kiln, and the whole mountain quaked greatly.
And as the sound of the trumpet grew louder
and louder, Moses spoke, and God answered
him in thunder. And the Lord came down upon
Mount Sinai, to the top of the mountain; and the
Lord called Moses to the top of the mountain,
and Moses went up. And the Lord said to Moses,
"Go down and warn the people, lest they break
through to the Lord to gaze and many of them
perish." (Ex 19:16–21)

Why was it terrifying and dangerous for the people at
Mt. Sinai when God "appeared" to them in the theoph-
any and revealed his Law? Because, as Blessed John
Henry Newman put it so exquisitely, in God's absolute
clarity, he *sees* who we *are*, and in him who is utterly
transparent, we see ourselves as we really are too:

Each of us must come to the evening of life.
Each of us must enter on eternity. Each of us
must come to that quiet, awful time, when we
will appear before the Lord of the vineyard, and
answer for the deeds done in the body, whether
they be good or bad. That, my dear brethren, you
will have to undergo. . . . It will be the dread
moment of expectation when your fate for eternity is in the balance, and when you are about to
be sent forth as the companion of either saints or
devils, without possibility of change. There can
be no change; there can be no reversal. As that
judgment decides it, so it will be for ever and
ever. Such is the particular judgment . . . when
we find ourselves by ourselves, one by one, in

his presence, and have brought before us most
vividly all the thoughts, words, and deeds of this
past life. Who will be able to bear the sight of
himself?

And yet we shall be obliged steadily to confront ourselves and to see ourselves. In this life
we shrink from knowing our real selves. We do
not like to know how sinful we are. We love those
who prophecy smooth things to us, and we are
angry with those who tell us of our faults. But on
that day, not one fault only, but all the secret, as
well as evident, defects of our character will be
clearly brought out. We shall see what we feared
to see here, and much more. And then, when the
full sight of ourselves comes to us, who will not
wish that he had known more of himself here,
rather than leaving it for the inevitable day to
reveal it all to him![2]

The more different from God we are, the more terrifying he is to us. The less similar our wills and our love,
the more fake we are and the more terrible the experience of his seeing through us is. He insists, "You shall
be holy, for I am holy" (1 Pt 1:16). A relationship with
him who *is*, by absolute necessity, must be founded on
transparency. I must be who I am in I AM's presence, or
I cannot know him for who he is and we cannot be one.

This holy transparency is why the Jews called I AM
WHO I AM the excellent name, the great name, the only
name, the glorious and terrible name, the hidden and
mysterious name, the name of the substance, the proper
name, and most frequently the explicit or the separated
name.

God calls us to complete transparency by revealing
us to ourselves in his Word. As he reveals himself to

us in his Word, we see ourselves and our dignity more clearly. The more obedient to that Word we are, the more holy we become, until we are so transparent that others can see him in us. The alternative is simply to devolve and feint into deeper fears and pretenses.

Phonies and Fakes

One of the clearest, most tragic examples of fakeness in the scriptures is the combative exchange the Pharisees initiate with Jesus in John 8. At issue is the Pharisees' denial of their slavery to fear and sin. Using Abraham as an example of holy transparency, Jesus calls out their fakeness and likens them to Satan himself, in the way they pretend to be holy but conceal dark deeds and darker hearts. "Abraham did not do this," he says, and they are enraged.

Although he only had two physical sons, Abraham's name means *father of many*. Over and over God revealed more and more of himself to Abraham, thereby revealing more and more of Abraham to himself, until after forty years or so of purification and struggle, he was transformed into the likeness of God so completely that he was willing to sacrifice his only son. Abraham became holy, effacing fully into the "is-ness" of his true dignity and his calling as the father of us all, in the consuming fires of God's transparent love.

"If you were Abraham's children, you would do what Abraham did," Jesus says to us as he told the Pharisees, calling them to see themselves as he saw them (Jn 8:39). They refused to acknowledge or confess to I AM the reality of who they were. Do I?

"God is not man, that he should lie" (Nm 23:19), so "it is impossible that God should prove false" (Heb 6:18);

HE IS WHO HE IS. Jesus, truth personified, would say to the Pharisees that when the tempter lies, "he speaks according to his own nature, for he is a liar and the father of lies" (Jn 8:44), meaning he is inherently all false and the source of all falseness. Satan deals in what things are not, in unreality. The term *lie*, here and in Eden, is not so much lying outright with words but lying with subtlety, pretense, deception, or fakeness. You know; it's that hairsplitting "it depends on what the meaning of the word 'is' is," or maybe what it is not.

The Living Not

Experienced exorcist Malachi Martin said,

> No one wants to believe in evil, really, above all, not in an evil being, an evil spirit. Everyone wants to abolish the idea. To admit the existence of evil means a responsibility, and no one wants that responsibility. That is the opening through which the evil spirit crawls, stilling all suspicions, making everything seem normal and natural. This is the "thought," the unwariness of the ordinary human being which amounts to a disinclination to believe in evil. And if you do not believe in evil, how can you believe in or ever know what good is?[3]

We contemplated I AM first because it is said that one can only understand evil after one understands good. If the essence of God is all he is, the essence of Satan is all he is not. Similarly, evil is the essence of all that is not and not a thing in itself, as darkness is the absence of light and not a thing in itself.

According to our philosophers and theologians, a thing is good in proportion that it possesses being. Because to exist is better than not to exist, "all being is good," so that God could look at everything to which he gave being, "and behold, it was very good" (Gn 1:31) precisely because it was connected to him and existing in unhindered potential according to its capability. Everything brought into being brimmed with good to the rim of its capacity.[4]

Hairsplitting though their precision may sound to my amateur sensibilities, God alone is essential being, so he alone is essentially and perfectly good. Everything else possesses limited being, and insofar as it does, it can be considered good. As far as a thing has reached its potential, it is as good as it is possible for it to be, so it is good in that measure.

Evil implies a deficiency in reaching full potential, so it cannot exist in God who is being itself and therefore fully good and the source of all potential. Evil can only exist in finite beings because they are necessarily limited and their potential can be further limited. Evil, then, is a deprivation of goodness; the essence of evil is failure. Evil is absence of good in a being that should possess that good.[5]

For example, that a person cannot see ultraviolet light is not evil, because the nature of the eye is such that it is physically incapable of doing so. But a person's blindness to the visible spectrum of light is a type of evil, because the human eye has the potential to and the capacity to see natural light. Blindness in a person is "evil" because by nature a human body has the potential to see. This is a kind of *natural* evil as opposed to *moral* evil, which involves personal culpability.

Because sin disconnects being from the source of its potential, God himself, it is evil. "The wages of sin is death" (Rom 6:23), so that a "little" death is inherent in even a "little" sin. There is no need whatsoever for God to "get even" or extraneously punish for sin when "one is punished by the very things by which he sins" (Wis 11:16). Do you see, then, why part of the actual definition of sin is forfeit? Because I can limit my own potential, I am capable of evil.

Evil can largely be described as the sum of opposition to a thing's dignity and potential. Like all biblical names, Satan's name, meaning *adversary* or *opponent* (Mt 4:10), tells us about his character. Satan has assumed this oppositional role both for himself and for all being.

Oddly, because Satan exists he is somehow good: all being is good by virtue of God as its origin. This very moment, Satan and all the demons exist only because God sustains them in being. This life force is his love. Though they and those in hell, by their own irrevocable choice, are incapable of returning God's love, he still loves them as his creatures and also sustains *them* in being. He does not destroy what he has made. If Satan were fully "ungood," he would not exist at all.

His existence, then, as a creature loved by God is the source of Satan's hatred: because God can take even his evil opposition and turn it for good, Satan is a servant to God even through that evil. Isn't that spectacularly *spectacular*?

Satan can no longer desire to be all God made and willed him to be. Sin irrevocably eliminated that will and ability. Since suffering exists in equal measure as the opposition to full potential, Satan suffers greatly because his unreached potential is so great. This is true for all of us, each in our own way.

Tidings of Great Joy

On the other hand, freedom is the ability to thrive according to one's nature. Grave sin, separation from or lack of God, makes me unfree because I am unable to live according to my truest nature anymore. That's why Jesus told the Pharisees that if they would abide in the truth, in him, they would be reconnected to God, their primary source, and be "free," free to conform to their inherent dignity and fulfill their complete potential.

But grace, ah, grace. The restoration of humankind's freedom began with the Incarnation, but Jesus did not simply reconnect us to our Source. Jesus came to give us *more* than the life of Eden. In him we have abundant life (Jn 10:10). He showed us what living *beyond* potential looks like. Grace *increases* or expands potential, the capacity for God. If there is no limit to grace, where might the limit be to my spiritual potential, besides the number of my days and my willingness to cooperate?

Often we assume Jesus performed miracles solely out of his divinity, and they seem somehow less spectacular for it. But Jesus' Incarnation was a willingness to limit himself in the physical ways we are limited, while living in full, unbroken connection to the Source and at the fullest human potential. Jesus was a model of what is possible in God: "Truly, truly, I say to you, he who believes in me will also do the works that I do; and greater works than these will he do, because I go to the Father" (Jn 14:12).

How is that even possible? So *wonderful* is the sense of hallelujah that fizzes in my heart at this reality that writing about it almost makes me burst!

As Thomas Aquinas said, God allows evil because in some mysterious way it can bring us closer to our full potential and to the desires of our heart, even if it doesn't seem that way at first. But he also admits that no philosophy of evil and suffering is sufficient to package it neatly.

Suffering remains a mystery. Just because we have a theology of suffering we are not released from the responsibility to attempt its alleviation insofar as we can. But when suffering is inescapable, I can rest in the knowledge that "in everything God works for good" (Rom 8:28).

The Walking Wounded

As our *adversary* and *opponent*, Satan uses our suffering to keep us enslaved to unforgiveness and fear and to prevent our reaching God fully in love. Woundedness and suffering is the most common entry point for Satan because it is usually where our deepest, most long-lasting fears were implanted. Doctors and theologians of the Church tell us that woundedness is the weakest point of the soul and usually the seat of the predominant fault. Satan ruthlessly exploits this area in order to lead us to despair and decadence. The great spiritual director Father Reginald Garrigou-Lagrange highlighted the predominant fault:

> It is of primary importance that we recognize our predominant fault and have no illusions about it. This is so much the more necessary as our adversary, the enemy of our soul, knows it quite well and makes use of it to stir up trouble in and about us . . . the predominant fault is the weak spot. . . . The enemy of souls seeks exactly this

easily vulnerable point in each one, and he finds
it without difficulty. Therefore we must recognize
it also.[6]

Each of us is wounded in one way or another,
whether as a result of personal sin, trauma, divorce,
death, or abandonment, and this woundedness is
expressed as fear, depression, anxiety, addiction, obses-
sions, compulsions, perfectionism, and all manner of
human ill. Woundedness originates from a lack of love.
In most cases the lack of love is perceived—from God,
parents, a spouse, friends, and so forth—regardless of
whether or not we are or were actually loved. Because,
according to psychologists, intense emotion imprints
memory, we blot out, ignore, or misinterpret expres-
sions of love we actually did receive and cling to a distorted notion that we are not loved so that the perception
becomes our darkened and sometimes false "reality."

Because God is love, when I experience a lack of
love, I am really experiencing a lack of God. This experience is perceived, not actual, because if God did not
love me, I would not exist: this is the irrefutable dignity
of every person.

There can be no actual experience of the absence of
God, because it is God's love that brought me into being
and sustains me: "In him we live and move and have
our being" (Acts 17:28). *This*, Dear One, is a feint of the
evil one, to make you believe you are lacking in love,
that you do not deserve love, that you are unlovable, or
that you are worthless. The mystic Julian of Norwich
understands: "Often our trust is not full. We are not certain that God hears us because we consider ourselves
worthless and as nothing. This is ridiculous and the
cause of our weakness. I have felt this way myself."[7]

His Eye Is on the Sparrow

We live out in the country on a little farm with a creek and a bit of land, and we all enjoy watching the families of bluebirds that nest in the numbers of boxes that my husband and boys built and placed around our property. Witnessing the first flights of baby bluebirds from my rocking chair on the porch is truly a lesson in the gentle persistence of God's love in coaxing us to fly, but the mild nature of bluebirds is also an invitation to predators, insects, and other birds to plunder their boxes and take over their nests. Sparrows, in particular, are the earliest spring invaders, perching atop the bluebird boxes and squawking interminably as they pop in and out of the bluebird holes and torment the birds inside until they just get tired and leave.

My husband makes vigilance for the protection of the bluebird boxes a serious priority. So there have been many occasions when sparrows have been unceremoniously blown off a bluebird box by his shotgun. Yes, folks, every one of our bluebird boxes is pockmarked, as is my heart from the repeated shock of hearing the gun go off with no warning.

Simultaneously, Bible reading and discussion have always been the first subject of our homeschool day in order to instill the habit from my boys' earliest years. When one of my sons was six or so, we were reading one of my favorite passages for meditation when I am feeling maudlin or afraid, or when I need to remind myself of the truth that God loves me tenderly: "Are not two sparrows sold for a penny? And not one of them will fall to the ground without your Father's will. But even the hairs of your head are all numbered. Fear not, therefore; you are of more value than many sparrows"

(Mt 10:29–31). I was enthusiastically encouraging my
son to trust in God's love and protection during our
school day, since he takes such care with even the sparrows, and he looked at me with eyes like dinner plates
and said, "But Daddy shoots 'em!"

Ahem. Dreadful illustration was that. But I hope
you will remember its humor when you are in the grip
of anxiety and worry. I know the passage is long, but
please read every word. Let it sink into your tired, fearful, frazzled heart.

> Therefore I tell you, do not be anxious about your
> life, what you shall eat or what you shall drink,
> nor about your body, what you shall put on. Is
> not life more than food, and the body more than
> clothing? Look at the birds of the air: they neither
> sow nor reap nor gather into barns, and yet your
> heavenly Father feeds them. Are you not of more
> value than they? And which of you by being anx-
> ious can add one cubit to his span of life? And
> why are you anxious about clothing? Consider
> the lilies of the field, how they grow; they neither
> toil nor spin; yet I tell you, even Solomon in all
> his glory was not clothed like one of these. But
> if God so clothes the grass of the field, which
> today is alive and tomorrow is thrown into the
> oven, will he not much more clothe you, O you
> of little faith?
>
> Therefore do not be anxious, saying, "What
> shall we eat?" or "What shall we drink?" or
> "What shall we wear?" For the Gentiles seek all
> these things; and your heavenly Father knows
> that you need them all. But seek first his kingdom
> and his righteousness, and all these things shall
> be yours as well. Therefore do not be anxious

about tomorrow, for tomorrow will be anxious
for itself. Let the day's own trouble be sufficient
for the day. (Mt 6:25–34)

This sounds as if it applies simply to the stuff and matter
of life, but I like to consider a much wider application
of emotional and spiritual needs too. After all, my "real
life" is the same as my "spiritual life"; it's all one life. If a
little sparrow is worth God's love and attention, I know
I cannot be worthless. "His eye is on the sparrow, and I
know He watches me."[8]

And I Know He Watches Me

My father's critical spirit and aggressive parenting style
instilled a deep experience of badness in me that made
me feel unloved and unlovable. The only attention I
seemed able to generate was negative, so I acted out.
Particularly in the weeks upon weeks of restriction and
silent treatment while his face and warmth were turned
away from me, I felt the isolation and darkness of being
unloved because of my badness (a long-term result has
been an ongoing terror of darkness and silence from
God in prayer, but that's another abandonment story). I
found that any good attention was conditional on good
behavior and performance, which I was unable to maintain, and was unrelated to who I *was*. As a child, this
feeling of being unloved motivated all my own lying,
deception, and misbehavior.

As an adult who left lying behind but still felt
unloved, I developed problems with rage (rebellion is
my predominant fault),[9] depression, addictions, and
hosts of other sins in an outward grasping for anything
that made me feel powerful or happy. Do you see how

my woundedness led to my predominant fault and was the entry point for Satan to exploit my pain and cause even more separation from God, the source of love?

I don't know about you, but the wound in my soul was a gaping, ravenous abyss of need. Nothing finite could fill it then, and nothing finite can fill it now. Only Jesus can satisfy the soul. As I began learning to live consciously in his love, I experienced round after round of painful circumstances that probed my woundedness and provoked my predominant fault. Satan exploited my wounds in innumerable, excruciating, creative ways.

But somehow, like GPS, God rerouted my anxious, fearful, depressed wrong turns back to the road that led straight into his arms. "For I am sure that neither death, nor life, nor angels, nor principalities, nor things present, nor things to come, nor powers, nor height, nor depth, nor anything else in all creation, will be able to separate us from the love of God in Christ Jesus our Lord" (Rom 8:38–39). Not even the evil feint of the devil against our dignity can separate us from God's love.

Belial

I hear it's typical of Italian families, but as I was growing up, my dad seemed always to be in a state of not speaking to somebody or other in his family. So when his brother died many years later, relatives my sister and I probably saw only a few times in our lifetimes all gathered at the funeral for the requisite burial and bridge building.

I have absolutely no recall of how it began, but in a private, conciliatory conversation with my father that night he related his regret for demanding I push my wedding date out and refusing to come at all or speak to me in the years since. Already a super-emotional time, I was elated to hear it and felt a piece of my world click into place. Grasping my hands warmly between his and leaning in so close I could smell the breath mint over his familiar cologne, he told me he had been so adamant, then, about my waiting to marry because he knew I could have been somebody.

I remember returning home in a fog. I was irritable and snappish—exhausted. I cried at the drop of a hat. I picked an enormous fight with my husband. For weeks I couldn't function normally, but I also couldn't figure out what was wrong with me. I remember writing in my prayer journal, "Why do I feel so *worthless*?" and gouging deep holes in the teary pages with my pen. I soaked my heavenly Father's divine lap. Why was I sad to the point of despair? Always faithful, God answered me.

Providentially, a friend and I were working through a Bible study on wellness of heart, soul, mind, and body; that week we were studying about emotions as the voice of relationships. I couldn't have been more stunned by the words on the page if they had leaped up and slapped me one by one: I was in the throes of a "historical emotion" meltdown.

Psychology tells us historical emotions are those that occurred earlier in life that are reexperienced later. A historical emotion has been felt repeatedly to the point that it takes up residence in the individual and lies dormant until she experiences events that reflect the earlier painful experience. At this point, the emotion is reactivated and reexperienced in a way that seems to bypass the will and conscience, and move her from feeling calm to inexplicably frantic in a matter of milliseconds. She might feel blindsided and wonder, *Where did that come from?* or *What was that?* Trying to make sense out of the feeling from a present perspective will only end in frustration, because the key is in the past.

In my mind I groped for the onset of the darkness and realized it was the funeral—that conversation. I could have been somebody.

But I wasn't.

You could have been somebody. But you're worthless. Do you feel that way?

That's a lie from the pit of hell, Dear One, the most pernicious, pervasive, evil lie Satan tells, and a hypocritical one as well.

Remember that biblical names reveal who a person *is*? At the same time as the insight into historical emotions, I was writing my own Bible study and discovered an interesting, frequently used biblical term that was a proper name in the context I was studying.

As I mentioned earlier in the chapter, I always look up biblical names, and this one absolutely stunned me: Belial. From two common Hebrew words *beli* (without) and *ya'al* (value), this word is usually translated as *worthless*, but later it became used as a personal name for Satan (2 Cor 6:15).

Belial accuses us with his own name.

Dear One, listen to me. If you get nothing else from this study, I pray with all my guts that you get this truth: you are loved. By virtue of your existence you are worthy of love. You are worthy *to be*.

More transparently than you can possibly endure, you are loved. He hides himself for you, not from you. He holds himself back from smothering you and overwhelming you completely with the heart-exploding love we call "heaven" because to see yourself in him, all at once, as transparently as he sees you would be beyond bearing. No one can see his face and live (Ex 33:20). He dwells in unapproachable light, whom no flesh has ever seen or can see (1 Tm 6:16).

The lie of worthlessness is the most vicious lie because it is an attack against the "is-ness," the inherent dignity of a person, that issues from all being; it bears the stench of sulfur and all the fury of worthlessness itself.

This is the lie Satan dares to tell each of us to exploit our shame and feelings of isolation from our own sin and from when we were sinned against, because he is worthlessness personified and he projects his own nothingness on all that is. Worthlessness is the most prevailing, successful after-sin feint of Satan against God's children. *Do. Not. Listen. To. This. Lie.*

Let's Review

- *A biblical name reveals who a person is.*

- *God's self-revealed name, I* AM, *confesses his desire to be known.*

- *God's name reveals him as the source of all being and his eternal,* covenantal relationship to humanity: I AM will be with his people.

- *With his everlasting name, God declares his eternal love for me*: I AM the God of Abraham, Isaac, and [your name].

- *God is a God of people,* not of things.

- *That I exist proves I am loved* by God and therefore worthy of love.

- *Evil is a lack of potential good* rather than a being itself.

- *My woundedness and suffering are the weak point* of my soul and the seat of my predominant fault.

- *Satan, meaning adversary, exploits my woundedness* and suffering with lies to keep me in fear and isolated from love.

- *One of Satan's most prevalent and powerful lies is that I am unlovable and worthless* unless I do something deserving of love.

- *Satan—also known as Belial—is, himself, worthless.*

- *My opponent Satan tempts me to fill the void of my woundedness* with anything other than God himself.

- *The truth is it can't be done.*

God Prompt

Right now, I'd like for you to get up and take this book with you to a bathroom or other private place with a mirror. Please do not read another word until you are standing in front of the mirror with the light on.

The psalmist says, "You formed my inward parts, you knitted me together in my mother's womb. . . . I am wondrously made. Wonderful are your works!" (Ps 139:13–14).

When you look in the mirror, what do you see? Do you, like the psalmist, see someone who is "wondrously made"? Does what you see make you want to sing or look away?

What did Jesus mean when he said to love others as we love ourselves? What is the you, the "is-ness" of you? Can you imagine your spirit without your body?

Stop to feel your pulse. Life is running through you. Life, being, is a gift from God, of his own breath. Feel your fingertips. Look at their pattern, a pattern shared with no other living being. You are uniquely, fearfully, and wonderfully made. You are made in God's image. You are loved for it.

Look again at the mirror. Ask God to show you the real you, the you without the image, the you that God sees.

You are loved. You *are*.

This is holy space. God is here. He welcomes you. You are embraced. This is your space to be with God and God's space to be with you. Make yourself at home. Be yourself. Be real. There's no rush. Let God love you.

Let God know you.

Let God touch you.

Let God speak to you.

Commune with him. Receive from him. When you are ready, move on to the prayer below, from Civilla D. Martin's hymn "His Eye Is on the Sparrow."

> Why should I feel discouraged, Why should the
>   shadows come,
> Why should my heart be lonely, And long for
>   heav'n and home,
> When Jesus is my portion, My constant Friend
>   is He;
> His eye is on the sparrow, And I know He
>   watches me.
>
> Chorus:
> I sing because I'm happy, I sing because I'm free;
> For His eye is on the sparrow, And I know He
>   watches me.
>
> "Let not your heart be troubled"; His tender
>   word I hear,
> And resting on His goodness, I lose my doubts
>   and fears,
> Tho' by the path He leadeth, but one step I may
>   see;

His eye is on the sparrow, And I know He
watches me.

Chorus

Whenever I am tempted, Whenever clouds arise,
When song gives place to sighing, When hope
within me dies,
I draw the closer to Him; From care He sets me
free;
His eye is on the sparrow, And I know He
watches me.[10]

An Invitation

*What was the most significant sentence, idea, or paragraph
you read in this chapter?* Was there any place that caused
a strong reaction of some kind—perhaps longing, perhaps anxiety, or perhaps a flash of insight? If anything
particularly struck you in this chapter, how is it the voice
of God, acting and moving in your heart and life?

*Talk to God about your woundedness, suffering, and
unforgiveness.* Regarding your woundedness and suffering, what are you most afraid of? Gathering and artic-
ulating may take considerable time, but please do not
rush. Try very hard not to numb the pain; the truth must
be completely felt to be completely healed. As you are
able to do so, privately talk with the Lord about what
you are discovering and trust him to guide you to heal
your soul and free you from the fear provoked by this
wound. Do not hold anything back from the Great Phy-
sician, who longs to heal you completely, because when
we deny our feelings we act them out.

Attempt to discern the lie. Have you begun to understand how Satan uses your wounds and unforgiveness
to tempt you to further sin? What is the lie he whispers

into your heart that provokes your predominant fault? How do you act out when you feel worthless? Can you name your worst behavior pattern or habit? See if you can identify the prevailing sin behind your behavior pattern: lust, gluttony, greed, jealousy, rebellion, anger, or fear? How often would you say acting on your habit or habits could be narrowed down to this prevailing fault?

Probe for the temptation. As you spend some time evaluating the history of your life in God's presence, what are you most frequently tempted with? Would you say this temptation is related to or triggered by a historical emotion?

Attempt to hear him speak through the Word. Which of the following verses speaks to you the most?

> We know that all things work for good for those who love God, who are called according to his purpose. (Rom 8:28, NABRE)

> You keep him in perfect peace, whose mind is stayed on thee, because he trusts in you. (Is 26:3)

> I sought the LORD, and He answered me, and delivered me from all my fears (Ps 34:4).

Did something in this verse, maybe just one word, attract you? What was it? Remembering you are in his presence, ask the Lord what he wants you to know through this verse. It might help to emphasize each word or phrase in turn.

Be ready for God's pop quizzes this week. If you undertake this kind of spiritual exercise with any sincerity or depth, you will probably be offered a pop quiz—a surprise temptation or test that involves the feeling of worthlessness—in the very near future. Please consider it a loving and fortuitous opportunity from the Holy

Spirit to practice what he is teaching, and not a punishment. He is teaching you to reject feelings of worthlessness and combat them with the truths you learned in this chapter. You may want to repeat the Let's Review section to yourself, or one of the verses that was particularly meaningful in this chapter, as you pray through the feelings in his presence.

I hope you will pray now for eyes to see and ears to hear the pop quiz for what it is when it comes. You may fail in the short term, until you become accustomed to recognizing the ways Satan exploits your woundedness, the lies you've been entertaining, your temptations, and your pop quizzes. I pray you will cling to the assurance of God's sure love for you and his promise to redeem your suffering. The process is necessarily slow and painful, but the fear will cease having any power once God has healed it.

PART 2

LOVE

WITH

ABANDON

5

$\mathcal{A}$ Fearless Desert

Advancing with Confidence

Once we've begun conquering our demons, we can advance with confidence. But—oh, joy—learning to love with abandon happens most effectively in the desert where we're stripped of everything we depend on. Its lonely austerity teaches us detachment, self-discipline, self-knowledge, and how to apply the strategies of spiritual warfare we've learned so far: battling temptation immediately and directly, practicing custody of the mind in our thoughts, and confronting lies with the truth of God's Word. Unfortunately, the desert is necessarily uncomfortable and we automatically chafe at its rigor, not realizing in our ignorance that resistance is fundamentally evil.

Because we reserve the word *evil* for things such as demonic possession, pedophilia, and Auschwitz, so often as real, seasoned people of faith we subtly consider ourselves beyond the capability of "evil." I know I did. I worked in ministry, prayed and studied my Bible daily, and participated in church several times a week. Then one morning this passage leapt off the page at me: "Take care, brethren, lest there be in any of you an evil, unbelieving heart, leading you to fall away from the living God" (Heb 3:12).

I have practiced daily lectio divina (*holy reading* or "daily quiet time" in the scriptures) for more than twenty years; I know when God is using a passage to speak directly to me, so I was stunned and disturbed by the "implication" that I was personally in danger of *evil*, of an "unbelieving heart," and of "falling away" from God. Those are dire words, Dear One! Because my "evil" heart wasn't so much implied as stated straight out, I confess I was a little offended that God would "so rudely" apply that verse to me. Turns out that passage applies to all of us every day, but especially now in our unique moment of history.

It's Always Today

In the beginning of the Church almost all Christians were Jewish. The book of Hebrews was a letter written to Hebrew Christians who were considering a return to their familiar Jewish faith in the face of severe persecution and martyrdom.

The section in Hebrews that contains the verse above begins, "Therefore, as the Holy Spirit says . . ." and then quotes part of Psalm 95. Essentially this sentence is an exclamation mark on the fact that God himself is saying to us, for a third time, what follows through the author of Hebrews: he said it first in the original accounts in Exodus and Numbers, then in the Psalms, and then here as a partial quotation of Psalm 95 in the Letter to the Hebrews as part of our New Testament.

As when your mom says your first, middle, and last names and you know you had better heed whatever is said next, whenever an idea is repeated this way in the scriptures, especially when the emphasis spans both Testaments, God is saying, "Pay attention!" He is stressing the importance of something—about himself, his purposes, or his ways.

The quotation, which follows, is from Psalm 95, part of the wisdom genre of the Bible, and is a summary of the forty years' wilderness events from Exodus and Numbers. *Wilderness* is synonymous with *desert* in the Bible.

> Therefore, as the Holy Spirit says, "Today, when you hear his voice, do not harden your hearts as in the *rebellion*, on the day of testing in the *wilderness*, where your fathers put me to the test and saw my works for forty years. Therefore I was provoked with that generation, and said, 'They always go astray in their hearts; they have not known my ways.' As I swore in my wrath, 'They shall never enter my rest.'" Take care, brethren, lest there be in any of you an evil, unbelieving heart, leading you to fall away from the living God. (Heb 3:7–12, emphasis added)

Notice that God made the drastic prediction that his people would never enter the Promised Land of rest because they did not know God's desert ways and therefore went astray in their hearts. As I studied, the unease multiplied in my own heart because I was wandering in a strange season of life myself and sensed I might somehow be in danger of forfeiting rest too.

Remember that this letter was written to persecuted Christians, like our suffering brothers and sisters all over the world today. Because *"Today,* when you hear his voice, do not harden your hearts" means right now, the Holy Spirit is speaking to you and I this very moment too, saying essentially, "Listen carefully to me, now, and rest." Rest, Beloved, is the absence of fear.

I don't know about you, but if I can be fearless in the face of ISIS, future political and economic upheaval, and the religious contentions of our day and time in the Church, I want to be. Unbeknownst to me at the time that God applied this passage to me, I would soon experience upheaval, "persecution," and contention myself, and begin learning what it means to "rest" there without fear.

But I'm Not Tired

In a long wail of lament, my beloved non-Catholic church had just split for the second time in ten years. My husband and I had both been in leadership there, and we left the church for its ugly habit of division and rebellion among the members and hid among nine thousand people in a neighboring megachurch of the same denomination. Because the new church was almost an hour away from our home, it was difficult to attend several times a week as we were happily accustomed to, nor were we required to be at leadership meetings, choir practices, or planning committees between worship services at a church to which we didn't formally belong. Our church attendance was reduced from often eight or more hours a week to never more than two.

Accustomed to frequently using my spiritual gifts and familiar with the biblical mandate to do so, I felt bereft and useless, adrift in a sea of people even while it felt wonderfully odd to simply attend church rather than work, plan, and facilitate too. A mere handful of weeks of "rest," though, and I began to chafe at the lack of activity; I felt irresponsible and even disciplined by God, as though he had removed me from duty for some reason. He had, it turns out! He removed me all the way out of my cherished Baptist church into the Catholic Church.

This season of inactivity was about three years long altogether, my own personal Arabian desert (Gal 1:17–18) in which the Lord ultimately accomplished my conversion to Catholicism. As a resident of the Bible Belt in which Catholics are rarely even considered Christians, I experienced wave after wave of accusation and concern from family and friends over my full communion and embrace of Catholicism. I was also battling my own anxieties over being inactive in formal service to others.

Over and over as my daily readings spoke about rest, I resisted out of boredom and feelings of uselessness. I wanted to advance, not retreat. Trouble was, I had no confidence in *where* I should be advancing. I kept telling the Lord, "But I'm not tired! I don't need to rest!" After several weeks of this back and forth, the passage in Hebrews about the "evil, unbelieving heart" that leads to unrest popped up. So I began studying the context. How enlightening.

Angels' Food

The sea had split. The enemy was drowned. And now the problems began.

The newly liberated nation was supposed to be on the way to the Promised Land but was seemingly stranded instead in a scorching desert wilderness facing an unending landscape of uncertainties. Taskmasters no longer responded to their cries—God did. In his infinite wisdom the Lord began our basic lessons in fearless living in the desert, through our daily fare, responding with protection and shelter on every level. But his people did not know his strange ways; they were restless and scared.

An omen of problems to come, right away their need for food prevailed on them to murmur against their leader, Moses: "Would that we had died by the hand of the LORD in the land of Egypt, when we sat by the fleshpots and ate bread to the full; for you have brought us out into this wilderness to kill this whole assembly with hunger" (Ex 16:3). Fleshpots are stewpots full of meat. I don't know about you, but I can understand this reaction, as I am frequently in need of forgiveness for what I say in hunger.

The Lord responded with a miraculous and equally mysterious celestial gift. A special, nutrient-complete "bread" rained from the heavens and appeared on the desert floor, ready to eat—the first fast food.

The people accepted it with piqued curiosity (Ex 16). Although the dew-covered bits satiated their hunger, they were unsure what it was exactly. They named it *manna*, meaning, *what is it?* Enough manna fell daily for each person with a double portion the day before the Sabbath, on which no manna fell. The people were able to eat it immediately or prepare it by baking or boiling. Any unused portion developed worms and spoiled by the next day.

Because it fell miraculously from "heaven," it became known as angels' food (Ps 78:25). Flakes as fine as frost, sweet as honey, and similar to the spice we know as coriander, it was kind of licorice-y, but don't worry; manna, "ministering to the desire of the one who took it, was changed to suit every one's liking" (Wis 16:21).

Ancient Jewish Talmud writings state that the taste of the manna was linked to the taster's thoughts.[1] Imagine it: Whatever taste you wanted, manna provided. You feel like steak? Your manna tastes like steak. Craving fudge cake? Voila, your manna is chocolate flavored.

Jesus illustrated and taught that the Old Testament manna prefigured the Eucharist (Jn 6), the bread from heaven in his own Body that he gave us at the Last Supper. He taught us to pray for it: "Give us this day our daily bread."

Aren't "this day" and "daily" redundant? In the Greek they are two different terms. "This day" means today, while "daily" is *epiousia* in Greek: *epi-* meaning *over, above, super*; and *-ousia* meaning *existence, essence, subsistence*. He means supersubstantial bread (Vulgate), superbeing bread, and hyperessence bread. He means the Eucharist, as the Church Fathers nearly unanimously agree.[2] And the Church has long referred to the eucharistic meal itself as "the bread of angels" (*panis angelicus*).

Like the thoughts the Israelites put into the manna that determined the taste that came out of it, doesn't my disposition going into Mass affect the benefit of the Eucharist to my soul and life? Do I gather from my weekly work and prepare for the Eucharist with the puzzled question in mind, "What is it?" Life presents me many opportunities for faith. Why not challenge my uncertainties with an exclamation: "It is what!" I can complain about my hunger for meaning, or I can accept these moments of challenge as God's provision and see, smell, and taste their sweetness so that the mysterious, daily miracle does not become empty.

Sold Out

Part of the discipline inherent in the manna was its one-day shelf life. There was no storing or hoarding it, because within twenty-four hours it bred worms and rotted anyway. By manna's nature, relying on God for their daily bread was compulsory for the Israelites. The people were at God's mercy for survival. They always had been, but it was in the desert that they truly came to know it. And unless we develop the discipline ourselves, it's in the desert, where God removes our attachments to financial security and comfort, that we learn it too.

One of the great strengths of denominationalism is its emphasis on biblical tithing. There is a powerful spiritual ethic at work in giving and tithing. For teaching us about who God is and what he is like, I have found no substitute.

Here in the West we rarely worry about where our next meal is coming from, but in uncertain economic times we might worry about the next paycheck. Tithing the local church on gross income seems grossly extravagant. What are they going to do with it anyway? Maybe I already give through my time, my talents, or my taxes, or to some charity of my choice (even if only once or twice a year).

All I can say to that is, I dare you. I dare you to attempt to outgive God in any area, but especially in tithing and almsgiving. "I have been young, and now am old; yet I have not seen the righteous forsaken or his children begging bread. He is ever giving liberally and lending, and his children become a blessing" (Ps 37:25–26).

This is often a huge area of neglect for us Catholics. We're like the rich young ruler that came to Jesus wanting all God had for him. Jesus told him to give all he had to God. Why does he do that? Does Jesus not like rich people? Does he require that those with means sell it all and give it away? Yes, he does, if it captures our hearts and hinders us from giving ourselves and our all to him.

But Jesus didn't tell rich people to give away all they have; he told a specific rich man to do so. Perhaps he did it because the young man was diseased, infected, and sick in his soul with his love of possessions and money and the illusion of security it lends. If the young man wanted all that Jesus could give, then he needed to give Jesus all that he had. Jesus was calling for him to be "sold out" for him. In fact, Jesus did that repeatedly to everyone who wanted to follow him. He always calls his followers to be sold out for him.

Everything in our bank account is God's. We "give" him a portion in tithes, but it's all his. One major health issue could occur, and it would all be gone. My car, my house, my clothes, and my children are all his. When I understand it is all his, I am no longer afraid, worried, anxious, or depressed about doing without whatever it is I have convinced myself I need (such as a rewards credit card and more books). I invite him to use them; I obey hilariously when he asks me to share.

The Bible condemns the Israelites repeatedly for testing God by complaining about their circumstances rather than relying on God for them. And yet, tithing on our daily bread, our income, is one case in which we are invited to "test God," as we see in this passage from Malachi: "Will man rob God? Yet you are robbing me. But you say, 'How are we robbing you?' In your tithes and offerings. . . . Bring the full tithes into the storehouse, that there may be food in my house; and thereby put me to the test, says the LORD of hosts, if I will not open the windows of heaven for you and pour down for you an overflowing blessing. I will rebuke the devourer for you, so that it will not destroy the fruits of your soil" (Mal 3:8–11).

The "devourer" or "destroyer" is anything that steals the seed, destroys the blade, sabotages with weeds, and consumes the crop—famine, insect, or enemy—and is actually a proper name for Satan that we'll talk about in the DVDs (Rv 9:11). Dear One, you can't advance in confidence if you're suspicious or terrified that God won't provide for you, because your effort and attention will always be toward your physical needs rather than the miraculous way forward. And don't you learn to trust his provision in the scarcity of desert giving and receiving?

Try him. You can't outgive him. I promise. I've tried it.

Eve Likes Her Pretty Baubles

My mother once gave me a Maltese cross studded with green, yellow, and brown crystals on a leather choker. I am wearing it in the header picture of my website where I am leaning against the ivy-covered wall.[3] Its old-world look was beautiful, and the necklace wasn't expensive, but it was a gift from my mother and I cherished it.

A young friend of mine admired it every time I wore it, and as I preened one day under her admiration I clearly felt God ask me to give it to her. I balked. I loved that necklace! It was a gift from my mother for Pete's sake! Every time my friend told me how pretty it was, I felt the twinge of guilt that I hadn't given God what he asked for. Every morning in prayer he brought it up.

I finally told him I simply didn't want to give it to her, and he asked me why. I kept trying to make it about being a gift from my mother, but we both knew that wasn't the real reason. The truth is I just loved it. It was mine, I had a right to it, and it was pretty. He asked me why he wasn't worth it. And then I caved. Because he really, truly is worth it—worth anything, worth everything. He is worth all I am, all I have, all I can be, all I ever will be.

I wrapped the little gift and carried it around for a couple of weeks hoping to run into her, and by the time I did I couldn't wait for her to have it. The day after I gave it away, I experienced a specific spiritual breakthrough that I had been praying for, and I know my possessiveness had been standing in the way of that grace all along. If you're not sure whether your possessions possess you, examine how you feel about giving them away. God cannot be exceeded in generosity, and tithing on our "manna" is the master teacher of that reality.

Streams in the Desert

Shortly into the Israelites' journey across the desert to the Promised Land, their water supply from Egypt was exhausted (Ex 17:1–7), a challenge that proved a constant test of Israel's peace. Even after the daily manna miracle, rather than simply ask patiently for water in faith, the people complained and murmured among themselves against Moses about the lack of water. "Why did you bring us up out of Egypt, to kill us and our children and our cattle with thirst?" (Ex 17:3).

Given that one can only survive three days without water, irritability seems a natural response to thirst in a desert, don't you think? I admit that God's making these poor former slaves ask for what he already knew they needed bugged me, but only until he shared that it was simply because he wanted them to be near him in their hearts. He wants us to need and ask, because he wants to be close.

God provided enough water for more than two million people and all their livestock out of a rock that followed them through the desert.

You read that right. The only available water source in the wilderness, according to the Fathers, "it was no motionless rock which followed the people."[4] Tertullian called this water-rock their "companion" and said, "This is the water which flowed from the rock which accompanied the people."[5] This water-giving rock followed them miraculously through the desert as a type of Christ-life-spring (1 Cor 10:1–4). But their constant protesting earned the incident two infamous proper names: Meribah, meaning *rebellion*, and Massah, meaning *wilderness* (Ps 95:7–11). Moses named the event so because the people "tempted God" there, asking, "Is the LORD among us or not?" (Ex 17:7), which is a sort of snide accusation of negligence.

Jesus, the model desert-negotiator, is always reminding us that we, also, must take up our daily crosses and be crucified with him at the hands of others and in service to them for love of him. With this law of love of the new covenant (Rom 13:8–10) comes the Holy Spirit's fountain of living water, our refreshment and restoration, and the rushing, flowing, moving, springing, redeeming, musical, quenching water of life (Jn 4) offered to us in the scriptures and in the sacraments of the Church.

I'll be honest; I get this lesson straight from God because I need it regularly. So if you chafe and complain against the dryness and weariness of the desert wilderness when you find yourself there, well, we'll persevere together. Let's encourage one another to draw from the well of living water flowing from the riven side of Christ, our stricken Rock. And how about reminding me, as we're advancing along our way, about those graves of the craving?

Graves of the Craving

The tone of voice, the petulance, and the knee-jerk reaction to scarcity and need is all too familiar by now. In another incident that ends with an explanation of the proper name given the place, the people complain of a lack of spice in their diet (Nm 11). They had no savory "thoughts" whatsoever of the manna, because they developed a "strong craving" for variety. Weeping like toddlers, they whine, "O that we had meat to eat! We remember the fish we ate in Egypt for nothing, the cucumbers, the melons, the leeks, the onions, and the garlic; but now our strength is dried up, and there is nothing at all but this manna to look at" (Nm 11:4–6).

The attitude was contemptuous, and Moses was discouraged to the point of death at the prospect that he should somehow provide meat for the multitude, so he neglected to intercede for them. Moses did not ask for help in leadership, and the people did not ask for meat or anything else in faith. Instead, they grumbled and complained at their lot, wailing in exaggeration that their souls were "dried up" from deprivation of rich food.

The fare in Egypt had been succulently seasoned and varied, even for slaves and the poor. The miraculous but comparatively plain manna had quickly grown monotonous. The people were sick of it so that

they seemed more willing to reject their deliverance
and return to slavery than endure deprivation in the
wilderness for the time it took to get from Egypt to the
Promised Land flowing with milk and honey.

What happens next reminds me of the scene in *The
Lord of the Rings* when Bilbo accuses Gandalf of wanting
the ring for himself. Gandalf raises to his full height
amid gathering shadows: "Do not take me for some
conjuror of cheap tricks! I am not trying to rob you. I'm
trying to help you!"[6]

Essentially God does something similar in response
to the Israelites' complaints: "You shall eat meat; for you
have wept in the hearing of the Lord, saying, 'Who will
give us meat to eat? For it was well with us in Egypt.'
Therefore the Lord will give you meat, and you shall
eat. You shall not eat one day, or two days, or five days,
or ten days, or twenty days, but a whole month, until
it comes out at your nostrils and becomes loathsome to
you" (Nm 11:18–20).

Migrating coveys of quail fluttered by the millions
into the camp on the wind. The peoples' frenzied craving at a peak, they gorged themselves on wild game that
is thought to have been contaminated by a migratory
diet of particular plants that are harmless to fowl but
fatally poisonous to human consumption.[7] Thousands
died, and the place was named "Kibroth Hattaavah,"
meaning Graves of the Craving.

The Bible says that God sent the quail so the people would die. This type of Old Testament tone often
bothers people who are beginning to read and study the
Bible. Ancient people viewed everything that happened
as a direct result of God's action, whether good or bad.
We see Jesus offering a more complete view of suffering
and "bad" circumstances, especially in John 9 where he
heals the blind man.[8]

But it was the people's unbridled lust and hysteria for novelty that caused them to descend on the quail so voraciously and that ended in their deaths. It wasn't so much what God did to them as what they did to themselves. Had they been less lustful and more disciplined, they would have known the quail were poisonous, as it was a well-known fact, and still is in that area, that migrating quail often were so.

In any case, this episode begs the following question: Since hunger and thirst are needs, and God says he will provide all our needs, was it the fact that they hungered and thirsted that was so insulting and "evil," according to our original text in Hebrews 3?

Psalm 78 sheds more light on the event. We learn they demanded what was intended to be a gift; they insisted on "food of their fancy" (NKJV); they "tested God" by accusing him of stinginess and an inability or unwillingness to provide bread, water, and meat for them. We discover he did not "deprive" them of what they craved and gave them what they desired so fervently, but in their greed and consumption "their days were consumed in futility and their years in fear" (Ps 78:33, NKJV). This is a dire warning, Dear One.

Do I feel purposeless, empty, and unsatisfied? Am I living in pervasive anxiety or fear (*terror* in the RSVCE translation of Ps 78:33)? Is it because in my monotony I demanded and received what I desired rather than resting in God's provision for me or asking him in simple, quiet, trusting faith for what I needed or wanted?

Plenitude in Poverty

When the last economic recession hit, we went from two incomes to half of one while simultaneously incurring

an enormous medical debt. Our standard of living was
reduced to scarcity; we were eating from the church's
food pantry, heating with wood, and showering once a
week to cut electricity costs.

In our plunge from plenty to poverty I was terrified, but we kept looking to God for provision while
continuing to give, and he always sent miraculous gifts:
supermarket gift cards of small, but enormously helpful
amounts arrived monthly in the mail; the hospital wrote
off the remaining medical debt after our explanation of
five-dollar monthly payments and a plea for easement.

Like God's first children in their forty years in the
wilderness whose clothes and sandals never wore out
(Dt 29:5), we were amazed at how we thrived under
such poor circumstances. And even so, I reminisced
about being able to eat out weekly and remember feeling so sick of having to invent something palatable to
eat with hamburger several times a week. I longed to
be able to skip cooking and cleaning up the kitchen just
once!

I was whining and irritable when I requested it, I
admit, but I asked the Lord if he would let us go out to
eat. That weekend we got an unexpected dinner invitation with a family who wanted to treat us for helping
them. While I ate like a pig, I don't think I have since
enjoyed and savored a dinner out like I did that one.

You often do not have, Dear One, because you complain more than you humbly ask God (Jas 4:2–3).

Holy Macaroni

When my son was seven or eight he developed a bit of
pickiness and began complaining about what I served
for dinner. I was talking to God in morning prayer about

how to handle it effectively, but gently, when this same wilderness story appeared in the readings. I distinctly felt him drawing my attention to it. Realizing what he could mean took more than a few incredulous moments, but the idea almost made me laugh out loud. I am not necessarily ashamed of how gleefully I commenced the lesson. I went straight to the store and bought twelve boxes of my son's favorite food, enough for a week of meals.

When a bowl of macaroni and cheese appeared on the breakfast table, he could hardly believe his fortune and shoveled it in with relish. At lunch he looked at it a moment but ate it heartily too, under my innocent, gleaming gaze. At dinner, when we had baked chicken, rice, and broccoli (one of his favorite meals), he ate macaroni quietly with a sidelong glance at me and stifled longing for the food on the table. I could feel his questions, but he never said a word. At breakfast the next morning, though, the bowl sat untouched, and he looked at me uneasily without daring to ask.

Sympathetic to his plight, I volunteered the story of the quail and the Israelites and told him how ungrateful he sounded when he complained about what I served for dinner. Somehow I asked him if he wanted to eat macaroni until it came out of his nose without the guffaw bursting out of me, and that was the last time I ever heard that child complain about a meal—to this day. In the end I had to return ten boxes of macaroni and cheese to the store.

Desert Ways

There is no advancing in the Christian life except through the desert. We all experience seasons of wandering around in savage country, and you can bet that the devil intends to capitalize on our fear while we're there.

Do you see how the children of Israel were tempted in desert scarcity the same way as Adam and Eve were tempted in the Garden's plenty? Satan knows these temptations succeed because we rarely know we are being tempted to fear, to "evil unbelief" in God's provision, through our natural appetites, needs, and senses. Spiritual warfare, then, says one psychologist, "is clearly something carried out in the flesh of man."[9] The Bible agrees: "For all that is in the world, the lust of the flesh and the lust of the eyes and the pride of life, is not of the Father but is of the world" (1 Jn 2:16).

When the chips were down in the early Church, when Christians were forced into financial devastation and struggling to survive, when the establishment was trying to kill them and they were enduring religious upheaval, the Holy Spirit reminded the Hebrews to remember the wilderness desolation of their ancestors and the innumerable times he provided for his people there.

Like all those who have trod the road before us, the lonely aridity of the desert is where I too learn fearlessness in trusting him for all my needs and desires. In fact, there is no biblical person of heroic faith and no saint I have ever studied who did not spend a significant amount of time in the desert.

The children of Israel teach us that the desert can be a barren place of great temptation and fear. But from Jesus we learn the desert can also be a place of purposeful isolation and the removal of distractions, a place of calling and mission, and great graces.

The enemy uses the desert to tempt us to focus on the shortage. Satan lures us to the desert to weaken us and lead us to complaining and rebellion so we'll never follow God out of our fears to rest in his love. This is the "evil" the Letter to the Hebrews (3:12) is talking about. The Holy Spirit leads us to the desert to empty us of Egypt so he can fill us with the promise of himself. In God's plan, the desert is a time to engage in ascetical practices. We need the desert to teach us to be fearless so we can advance in confidence.

The Church Fathers distilled all our temptations to their essence and categorized them all as proceeding from the world, the flesh, and the devil. The Old Testament desert wanderings illustrate these categories perfectly and teach us important lessons on spiritual warfare, as we'll see again in chapter 8. In a scriptural sense, the desert is a contradiction. Every desert season presents an important choice: detach from the comforts of the world and learn to trust God, or yield to the flesh.

Necessarily, the desert is empty and comfortless: water and food (consolations) are scarce. There is no relief from the battering wind and heat of day, nor the unfiltered cold of night. The dunes seem unending and are stark and lonely. A metaphor for both life and death, the desert can be a place of hopelessness or one of purposeful contemplation and prayer. But the desert is actually God's primary training ground. It is in the desert that you become fearless and learn to trust with abandon; you should cling to this promise when you find yourself there.

Let's Review

- *The Holy Spirit adamantly encourages me in times of political, economic, and religious upheaval* to trust unconditionally in God's provision.

- *Rebellion = sin = lies = untrust = unbelief = unrest = fear = evil* (Heb 3:7–19)

- *Obedience = life = truth = trust = belief = love = rest = peace = FEARLESS*

- *When I am afraid to trust God's Word, I must make faith a matter of will and action* rather than emotion. My emotions will follow my will.

- *God did not directly prevent the Israelites' entry into the Promised Land of rest. The Israelites refused to enter out of fear* that God would not provide, proving they did not know or trust God's power, love, or generous ways.

- *God leads me to the desert to learn to trust him.*

- *Refusing to trust the timing, amount, or substance* of God's provision causes discontent, purposelessness, futility, and fear.

- *God may allow me to have what I demand or contrive in obstinacy,* but I will probably not like it once I get it.

- *Tithing helps protect me and what concerns me from my enemy because it teaches me to trust God with my money.*

- *I can never outgive God.* He will give me himself when I give him myself.

An Invitation

My three-year sabbatical in the desert, in which God warned me of an evil heart of unbelief and of going astray in my heart out of resistance to his leadership, was lonely, dry, and scary. I had no idea what to do or where I was spiritually, only that I was supposed to somehow "rest" in the uncertainty, darkness, and seeming deficiencies.

Looking back, it was ultimately the route to Catholicism and public ministry. Had I not learned to be fearless in the desert, I would not have had the spiritual chops to enter the Church of history, and I would have sacrificed my family and burned out in ministry after my full communion while I floundered in attempting to provide for myself there.

You know that old saying, "Do what you always do and you'll get what you always got"? I dislike suffering a great deal, so I have always preferred to learn from others' mistakes rather than make them myself. And when I discern I am about to enter the desert or am already knee-deep in sand, I always tell God I'll learn fast if he'll teach fast. Yet it has been in my wanderings and scarcities and in the roaring temptations there that I have learned that just between what is real and what is seen there is refuge in my Father's footsteps. I am fearless there. "Where the lion walks, I will not be afraid. My feet may touch the earth, but my heart is swept away."[10]

The most powerful experiences of God recorded in the scriptures almost always happen in the desert. If I can rest fearlessly in the discomfort long enough for it to do its work of detachment, might I experience God more powerfully than ever before and advance toward the future in confidence?

God Prompt

After the miraculous emancipation from slavery, parting of the Red Sea, pillar of fire and cloud that guided them, water gushing from the rock, and daily angels' food raining from the sky, the people demanded the "food of their fancy," and their obstinacy in having what they wanted ultimately killed them.

The Israelites' faults are used as a cautionary tale throughout the scriptures as examples of what not to do while following God through wilderness, desert, and persecution. I can't number the times I have heard people exclaim how stupid the Israelites were for doing the same wrong things over and over, as though we wouldn't act the way they did, complaining, whining, accusing, refusing, failing, and fearing—as though the Israelites are somehow not us.

What was the most significant sentence, idea, or paragraph you read in this chapter? Was there any place that caused a strong reaction of some kind—perhaps longing, anxiety, or a flash of insight? If anything particularly struck you in this chapter, how might the voice of God, acting and moving in your heart and life?

When have you blamed your church leaders for lack of freshness, spice, and meat in your spiritual diet? What is it about the way we mishandle our legitimate needs and desires that qualifies it as sin? What happens to us when we persist in rejecting God's provision for us, in the timing, the measure, or the substance?

Talk to God about your fears and worries in the current areas of need in your life. Do you have a hard time trusting God for provision in your life? Do you tithe regularly? Why or why not?

Attempt to discern the lie. I have found that desert temptations almost always provoke historical emotions and then trigger my predominant fault. Would you say you have experience with miswired emotions, or "historical emotions"? In God's presence, do your best to locate the time and place when you first felt the emotion. Ask yourself, *When and where have I felt like this before?* Have you begun to understand how Satan uses your legitimate needs to tempt you to knee-jerk sin reactions out of depletion, exhaustion, anger, or fear?

What is the lie he whispers into your heart when you have a need that you fear won't be met? What is the lie he whispers into your heart when you consider tithing?

Probe for the temptation. All my life I have heard people say that God is always on time, but I maintain he always arrives at the last darn minute. How long does it usually take in a situation of insufficiency before you begin to panic that he has not done something yet? Have you ever waited long enough without acting on your own that he finally did come through?

Attempt to hear him speak through the Word: St. Augustine said that fasting and almsgiving are "the two wings of prayer" that enable the soul to gain momentum and fly even to God.[11] Here is a selection of passages on almsgiving and tithing. As you consider the following verses in his presence, ask him to speak clearly to your heart.

> Consider how you have fared. You have sown much, and harvested little; you eat, but you never have enough; you drink, but you never have your fill; you clothe yourselves, but no one is warm; and he who earns wages earns wages to put them into a bag with holes. Thus says the LORD of hosts: Consider how you have fared. . . . You have looked for much, and behold, it came to little; and when you brought it home, I blew it away. Why? says the LORD of hosts. Because of my house that lies in ruins, while you busy yourselves each with his own house. (Hg 1:5–7, 9)

> I have been young, and now am old; yet I have not seen the righteous forsaken or his children begging bread. (Ps 37:25)

> One man gives freely, yet grows all the richer; another withholds what he should give, and only suffers want. The liberal man will be enriched, and one who waters will himself be watered. (Prv 11:24–25)

Bring the full tithes into the storehouse, that there may be food in my house; and thereby put me to the test, says the LORD of hosts, if I will not open the windows of heaven for you and pour down for you an overflowing blessing. (Mal 3:10)

But when you give alms, do not let your left hand know what your right hand is doing, so that your alms may be in secret; and your Father who sees in secret will reward you. (Mt 6:3–4)

No one can serve two masters; for either he will hate the one and love the other, or he will be devoted to the one and despise the other. You cannot serve God and mammon [money]. (Mt 6:24)

Truly I say to you, this poor widow put in more than all those who are contributing to the treasury. For they all contributed out of their abundance; but she out of her poverty has put in everything she had, her whole living. (Mk 12:43–44)

Give, and it will be given to you; good measure, pressed down, shaken together, running over, will be put into your lap. For the measure you give will be the measure you get back. (Lk 6:38)

For God so loved the world that he gave his only-begotten Son, that whoever believes in him should not perish but have eternal life. (Jn 3:16)

The point is this: he who sows sparingly will also reap sparingly, and he who sows bountifully will also reap bountifully. Each one must do just as he has made up his mind, not reluctantly or under compulsion, for God loves a cheerful giver. And

> God is able to provide you with every blessing in abundance, so that you may always have enough of everything and may provide in abundance for every good work. (2 Cor 9:6–8)

If you had to summarize all of these verses in one sentence, what would it be? Now that you believe fearlessly in God's absolute provision, let's see what weapons he provides for our protection in this valley of tears.

6

$\mathcal{F}$earless Resistance

Wielding Unworldly Weapons

God's Old Testament people were sent a deliverer in Moses and a conqueror in Joshua, but the people failed to clear out the Promised Land of all its evil influences and enemies, and eventually they were overtaken without settling all the territory they were given (Jgs 3:1–4). Doesn't the prosperity of the Promised Land always tempt me to distraction and self-medication rather than inspire me to battle on for more territory?

Is that why we get obnoxious over football games and enjoy fantasizing we are important and rich through the voyeurism of reality TV and awards shows? Who's wearing whose designer's gowns and jewels, the best and worst dressed, and more fashion "wins" and "fails" than you can shake a diamond stick at are obviously top priority to require four hours of the whole nation's prime time. What, exactly, is all my grasping at diversion meant to "divert" me from?

It's hard for me to enjoy stuff like that for more than about ten minutes, max. After three or four gowns or self-important interviews (rounded out with gratuitous propaganda), the "bread and circuses"[1] of it all starts to circle me like a mosquito.

And pretty soon I'm circling it like a dog chained to a stake, yanking on the idea that behind all the waltzing down red carpet and twirling in gardens of flashbulbs in borrowed emeralds and floor-length chiffon, the Hunger Games are raging for every one of those souls and my own.

Probably a less uptight me isn't haunted by imaginings of Judgment Day in which I, like Oskar Schindler, will mourn how my own hoarded, tightly possessed possessions, however invaluable or few, might have helped someone desperate to eat or live. She's perfectly happy "unthinking," flitting through the battle like so many numbers of mad dandies, singing and gathering up shrapnel thinking they're flowers.

Let's get real: Aren't distractions palliative? Doesn't every problem get worse the longer you ignore it? Wouldn't you rather *be* happy than *seem* happy? Don't diversions terminate our progress and delay preparation for the eternity beyond the silent, sunken mound and the stone with a few words on it? That old saying *You can't take it with you* is untrue. Everything you entrust to Jesus will be kept for eternity in him. What will you leave behind, undone, unrealized, unfulfilled, because you were unwilling to resist the onslaught of distractions and prepare it for eternity?

Attention!

As soon as the people left the desert and entered the Promised Land, they were confronted by the stronghold of Jericho. The city and the whole land was their possession by promise, but they still had to war and fight to make it their own. God warned Joshua that once he delivered Jericho's stronghold into their hands, they must not rebuild it (Jos 6:26) or it would overtake even their descendants.

Destroying strongholds means demolition of the patterns and ideas that hold me and my world in bondage, things I rationalize and justify, and places in my life and the world where Satan and demons hide and are protected—such as my consumerism, my politics, my apathy.

Yes, I went morose on you. Don't stone me. Every day that I open up my email account and see a Kardashian or three on the trending list, I almost vomit. Why are God's people giving inordinate amounts of their time and attention to this stuff? Is the time for parties while the battle rages or after the war is over? Will I be Marie Antoinette or Joan of Arc?

Does the craving for constant entertainment not create a mass grave of sleepers that dons paisley maxi dresses rather than the armor of God in the invisible war for souls and territory? "You who say, 'Today or tomorrow we will go into such and such a town and [go shopping and get stuff]'; whereas you do not know about tomorrow. What is your life? For you are a mist that appears for a little time and then vanishes" (Jas 4:13–14).

Luxury is not a virtue. Politics will not save the world or anyone in it. A cursory reading of the Old Testament reveals that the true prophets always call us away from that stuff.

Dear One, when life is a vapor there isn't much time to learn and live wisely. We are charged with "redeeming the time, because the days are evil" (Eph 5:16, DRB). Jesus also warns, if we exorcise the sin from our lives but fail to fill the void with righteousness, our last enslavement will be worse than the first (Lk 11:24–26).

How do we protect and preserve the spoils of victory that are rightfully ours in Christ? If "the weapons of our warfare are not worldly but have divine power to destroy strongholds" (2 Cor 10:3–4), what do we do when we live in the world but are not carrying on a worldly war? How do we resist the forces of evil in the middle of a parade of diversions?

Stand for Something or Fall for Anything

Be strong in the Lord and in the strength of his might. Put on the whole armor of God, that you may be able to *stand* against the wiles of the devil. For we are not contending against flesh and blood, but against the principalities, against the powers, against the world rulers of this present darkness, against the spiritual hosts of wickedness in the heavenly places. Therefore take the whole armor of God, that you may be able to *withstand* in the evil day, and having done all, to *stand*. (Eph 6:10–13, emphasis added)

Notice that we are not asked to fight offense. In fact, throughout the scriptures we are never encouraged to fight against Satan in an offensive way and are even *dis*couraged from doing so. He has had millennia of experience dealing with Eve.

St. Michael thought it prudent to leave Satan to God to handle; how much more should I? "But when the archangel Michael, contending with the devil, disputed about the body of Moses, he did not presume to pronounce a reviling judgment upon him, but said, 'The Lord rebuke you'" (Jude 1:9). St. Michael, like all angels, good or evil, understands authority. Satan is not under our authority, so we are not asked to engage him offensively. To do so is impotent, dangerous, and foolhardy, and those who attempt it apart from the full authority of Christ in his Church open themselves to serious spiritual attack.

And it's unnecessary: "Submit . . . to God. Resist the devil and he will flee from you" (Jas 4:7). Like Frodo who received a glittering mithril shirt, I am provided with a special, mysterious armor. All I have to do to put Satan on the run is stand my ground in this armor and let Jesus fight for me.

Armor of God

When St. Paul wrote his Letter to the Ephesians describing the armor of God, he said, "I am an ambassador in chains" (6:20). Under arrest and chained to a Roman soldier, his incarceration provided a unique opportunity to view closely one of the best trained and armed fighters in the world at that time, and the battle gear that every Roman soldier possessed. He applied his observations in a "spiritual" sense, using military imagery to describe the armor and weaponry that we need to defend ourselves against the evil influence of an unseen, threatening enemy. I hope you'll imagine yourself looking like Joan of Arc in each piece of this armor.

Part of the Roman armor was taken up only when the actual fighting was about to begin. But the first three pieces mentioned by St. Paul were never removed by the Roman soldier, and all conveniently begin with *B*: belt, breastplate, and boots. "Stand therefore, having fastened the belt of truth around your waist, and having put on the breastplate of righteousness, and having shod your feet with the equipment of the gospel of peace" (Eph 6:14–15 NRSV).

The first piece of armor is the belt of truth. Ancient daily garb for men and women included a long, ankle-length linen robe or tunic that Middle Easterners still wear today. Back in the days of the ancient East, a man wore a belt or girdle around his tunic. When he needed to run, work strenuously, or fight, he would "gird his loins." I've always found that an entertaining turn of phrase: loins . . . heh.

Like the Scottish kilt, heh, the tunic was comfortable and breezy around the loins, but its long hem interfered with fighting and hard labor. So when an ancient Hebrew man battled the Philistines, for instance, he lifted and tucked the hem into the girdle or tied it in a knot to keep it off the ground. This meant hiking the hem up to the thigh, pulling the robe snug against the backside, and gathering all the excess material in front. Then he passed the tail of the material through his legs to the rear like a diaper. He separated the material into two hands-full and tucked them into his belt on either side. I don't know about you, but I do something similar to this with my sundress when I weed my kitchen garden in the summer.

Basically, the effect was a pair of shorts that provided more freedom of movement and kept his clothes from clinging and hanging up. To say, "Gird up your loins," was to tell someone to get ready for hard work or battle, an ancient way of saying, "Man up!"

If the military imagery seems too masculine to identify with, remember that women are battle partners with the Holy Spirit. They are particularly called and gifted to struggle against evil and to prepare for the spiritual restoration of life. Dear One, we have to employ our girl power in cooperation with the Holy Spirit to love and lift all we've been given (Jn 17:6ff).

From a Roman's belt, wide enough to also offer protection from fatal stomach wounds, hung the sheath for his sword. The belt supported the back, the structure of the whole fighting system, to reduce strain and injury, and it covered the waist and bowels. We speak of having gut feelings. In the scriptures, the heart as the seat of emotions was usually rendered *bowels* in older translations (2 Cor 6:12; Col 3:12; 1 Jn 3:17, DRB).

St. Paul is saying, *Get ready. Strengthen your spiritual backbone. Protect your heart and emotions with truth.* This means avoiding fear and other emotional reactions to our trials, temptations, and spiritual assaults by interpreting emotion through truth, rather than vice versa. But it also means not giving place to the spiritual weakness of hypocrisy and fakeness. Holiness means authenticity, purity of heart, and single-minded pursuit of God. There is no substitute for scriptural truth to protect vulnerable emotions and develop a spiritual spine to help us bear the daily load.

When I married, I spent the first few months in a panic for my husband's safety. Conditioned by my father wound to expect the withholding or renege of anything I really loved or wanted due to my "badness," I held my breath as I waited in the back of the church for an earthquake to swallow us up before I could get down the aisle and through the I dos. For the first few weeks I was frozen until he got home or called, sure something awful had happened. I just knew God would use some clever, agonizing way to revoke this precious privilege that I so clearly did not deserve. To this day I call my husband my first gift because I've had him now for twenty-three wonderful years.

The belt of truth in the armor of God protects my emotions. I must know the truth about the intimate parts of myself, that which is led astray by doubt and passions through my predominant fault. Truth, not emotion, is my balance, support, and backbone for battle. For me, the truth is I have a father wound, and I can and must exercise self-control, truth, and self-knowledge in it, rather than allowing doubt to thrash me about "like a wave of the sea that is driven and tossed by the wind" (Jas 1:6).

Having Put on the Breastplate of Righteousness

Made of thick, hard leather, the breastplate defended the soft, internal organs. I remember in my childhood one of my father's fellow highway patrolmen died on a traffic stop because, although he had his gun, his handcuffs, and his nightstick, he had not worn his bulletproof vest, his breastplate.

Not all blows to the chest are fatal. A hit to the solar plexus can knock the wind out of you and bring you to your knees, leaving you temporarily unable to defend yourself. Ever had someone level a false accusation at you that left you stunned and disoriented?

The breastplate is "righteousness." At its barest, righteousness, or rightness, means no sin. Remember that Satan's only power against us is to influence us to sin. One sin, any sin, puts a breach in the breastplate, but a solid breastplate of righteousness is impenetrable.

At its fullest, righteousness is love. The demons believe, but they tremble because they do not love what they know (Jas 2:19). Because I love my neighbor, or because I love God when I can't love her, I do not sin against her. Like that return to Eden, to be right with

God is to love him with all our heart, soul, mind, and strength, and to love my neighbor as myself. When I do sin, though, righteousness means I am rightly related to God, self, and others through Confession and forgiveness. What do I mean?

I have a friend whose mother suffered a sudden, violent death. She told me recently that to this day, almost a decade and a half afterward, flashes of guilt overwhelm her concerning a sin she committed against her mother before she died. She said even though she knew it was Satan "throwing it in her face," it still hurts every time and makes her feel sick, worthless, and horrible every time.

But she also knows her position in Christ, that God forgives and forgets, casting our sins as far from him as the east is from the west (Ps 103:12), and she said that knowledge is her "weapon to fight Satan with." That weapon is her breastplate of righteousness: "There is therefore now no condemnation for those who are in Christ Jesus," those who walk in the Spirit and not in the sins of the flesh (Rom 8:1).

Dear One, do you struggle with guilt? Righteousness conquers guilt. "If we confess our sins, he is faithful and just, and will forgive our sins and cleanse us from all unrighteousness" (1 Jn 1:9). That's a promise that he will cleanse us of both the guilt and the sin when we follow him in righteousness.

Having Shod Your Feet with the Boots of Peace

The *caligae*, Roman military boots, were such important equipment that it has been said the soldiers' boots were the secret of the Roman conquest. Designed for long marches over every kind of rough terrain, they were three-inch, French, alligator-skinned couture heels. Ha! I was just making sure you were paying attention. Actually they were heavy-soled, open-toed, spiked cleats that laced up past the ankle for firm footing during hand-to-hand combat.

Through the roughest terrains of life, firm footing as a Christian involves fearlessness and peace. We no longer fight against God, turning our will against his. We understand and trust what the wise spiritual director Fr. Jean-Pierre de Caussade taught: "There is never a moment when God does not come forward in the guise of some suffering or duty. . . . The disclosure that each moment brings is of such great value because it is meant for us personally."[2]

Our sins do not separate us from God because we systematically eliminate them from our lives and seek and stand in his forgiveness. We are no longer afraid of him. We are reconciled: "In Christ God was reconciling the world to himself, not counting their trespasses against them, and entrusting to us the message of reconciliation" (2 Cor 5:19). We learn to trust and follow, faith to faith (Rom 1:17), and we find ourselves in a glorious love that is our peace. Good news for those of us who struggle with fear!

Peace in the scriptures is *shalom*, and it's synonymous with *salvation*. It's a great big, full, *fearless* word, meaning *integration, wholeness, fulfillment*, and *sanctification*. And *this* is why "the peace of God, which passes all understanding, will keep your hearts and your minds in Christ Jesus" (Phil 4:7).

Perhaps because we are crippled with depression, anxiety, and fear, we have forgotten what is so good about the Good News. Cardinal Joseph Ratzinger encouraged us, "Christ is 'God Who is near to us,' willing and able to liberate us: that is why the Gospel really

is 'Good News.' And that is why we must go on pro-
claiming Christ in those realms of fear and unfreedom."[3]
Firmly planted in the Good News of salvation peace,
we discover our beautiful feet: "How beautiful on the
mountains are the feet of him who brings good tidings"
(Is 52:7).

Taking the Shield of Faith

While the Roman soldier always wore the first three
pieces of armor, the next three were only taken up when
the actual fighting was about to begin: "above all, taking
the shield of faith, with which you can quench all the
flaming darts of the evil one. And take the helmet of
salvation, and the sword of the Spirit, which is the word
of God" (Eph 6:16–17).

One of the most dangerous weapons in ancient
warfare was the fiery dart. The heads were wrapped
with flax or hemp fiber, soaked in pitch, and then set
afire before being launched by the hundreds. Wooden
shields large enough to protect the entire body could
be set aflame by the arrows, so they were covered with
a layer of hide soaked in water before battle so that
even though fiery darts might pierce the shield, the fire
was quenched immediately. Imagine rows and rows of
advancing Roman soldiers with shields overlapped,
creating an enormous scalelike line behind impenetrable
plated mail.

The Bible says the shield in the armor of God is
faith—not faith in my faith, and not believing *in* God,
since the demons also believe (Jas 2:19), but believing
God himself.[4] Faith is believing what God says in his
Word; taking him at his Word and standing on that truth
no matter what; and more importantly, believing that he

is good, particularly when circumstances no longer feel good. That's true faith.

The flaming arrows of the enemy are lies and temptations, especially regarding our predominant fault, but also in our relationships, habits, circumstances, and desires, according to the *Catechism*:

> The Holy Spirit makes us discern between trials, which are necessary for the growth of the inner man, and temptation, which leads to sin and death. We must also discern between being tempted and consenting to temptation. Finally, discernment unmasks the lie of temptation, whose object appears to be good, a "delight to the eyes" and desirable, when in reality its fruit is death. God does not want to impose the good, but wants free beings. . . . There is a certain usefulness to temptation. No one but God knows what our soul has received from him, not even we ourselves. But temptation reveals it in order to teach us to know ourselves, and in this way we discover our evil inclinations [predominant fault] and are obliged to give thanks for the goods that temptation has revealed to us. (CCC, 2847–48)

The fiery darts of the enemy's temptations must be quenched before they burn through the shield, or worse, bore into our flesh because we have no shield.

One of the passages I quote to myself in times of stress, fear, or danger is "the Lord is my strength and my shield" and "rear guard" (Ps 28:7; Is 52:12). He goes before me and behind me, surrounding me with his presence and protection.

Take the Helmet of Salvation

The helmet protects the head, the womb of the thought life. Every temptation begins with the introduction of a thought seed, a lie, and an invitation to allow it and assist it to germinate (Jas 1:14–16). "For though we live in the world we are not carrying on a worldly war, for the weapons of our warfare are not worldly but have divine power to destroy strongholds [of sin]. We destroy arguments and every proud obstacle to the knowledge of God, and take every thought captive to obey Christ" (2 Cor 10:3–5).

While I was struggling to overcome my smoking habit, I discovered that all I thought about was smoking. Surely that was the physical addiction talking in the beginning. But after I had been cigarette-free for weeks and suddenly began to feel seriously harassed by thoughts of smoking again, well, that seemed to be something altogether different. I have found that entertaining those hordes of fiery darts, when they come, leads swiftly and directly to sin.

I am in control of what I think. This practice is sometimes called custody of the mind. Brain science tells us that interrupting and rerouting destructive or negative thought patterns reverses dulled physical and spiritual senses too, assisting in the formation of new, healthy behaviors.[5] How do I "take every thought captive"?

What do I do when thoughts assail me or I catch myself thinking along lines I want to avoid? What thoughts qualify to be in my mind? "Whatever is true, whatever is honorable, whatever is just, whatever is pure, whatever is lovely, whatever is gracious, if there is any excellence, if there is anything worthy of praise, think about these things" (Phil 4:8).

I admit it takes some practice, but once you are aware that your mind is headed down some futile road, stop yourself and divert your thoughts to something happy, peaceful, and constructive. Decide what your "redirect thoughts" will be ahead of time so you can go right to them.

Thoughts are like toddlers and kittens: you can't yell at them for exploring or explain why the answer to putting peas up their noses or eating the poisonous houseplant is no! You change their position and distract them with something else, and danger is averted. If you need help in catching the thoughts before you put the peas up your nose, then ask your guardian angel; our guardian angels *love* helping us with this stuff (Ps 91:11; Heb 1:14) because they obtain rewards with us.

Another strategy is praise. "Music is . . . acceleration in the rhythm of celestial experience" and "quite opaque" to devils, it is said in C. S. Lewis's *The Screwtape Letters.*[6] Lucifer was created with music in him (Ez 28:13–14). What does he do with that capacity now that his will is turned against God? Worship must be violently distasteful to him.

Praise and thank God for your blessings. Make a list of his gifts and your spiritual markers. Keep a running tally of your answered prayers. Nothing keeps me from sin like the fresh realization of God's constant care and provision.

Go to Mass, the highest form of worship. Play Gregorian chant or praise and worship music. Worship and sing, knowing the angels worship and sing with you (Is 6:3). In the battle for the stronghold of Jericho, God commanded his people to send the musicians into war first (Jos 6). The Bible tells us God inhabits the praises of his people so that it confuses and defeats the enemy (Ps 8:1–2, 149). "When they began to sing and praise, the

Lᴏʀᴅ set an ambush against the [enemy] . . . so that they were routed" (2 Chr 20:22). Sing praise! Sing, knowing he is present and that Satan must flee, and you will find your thoughts lifted from the quicksand of temptation.

The Sword of the Spirit

The Bible gives us one defensive weapon that is simultaneously used as the singular offensive weapon, "the sword of the Spirit, which is the word of God" (Eph 6:17). *Word* literally means *promise* or *command*, *to utter*, *pronounce*, or *speak*. Dear One, if you don't know the Word of God, if it doesn't drip from your tongue like honey, you have *no weapon* against a vile and violent spiritual enemy.

"For the word of God is living and active, sharper than any two-edged sword, piercing to the division of soul and spirit, of joints and marrow, and discerning the thoughts and intentions of the heart" (Heb 4:12).

We Catholics know the sacraments; we know the prayers; and we know the saints. But we do not know the scriptures: "My people are destroyed for lack of knowledge" (Hos 4:6). *Fearless* has focused on the scriptures because there is a plethora of resources on the subject of spiritual warfare from the perspective of sacraments and sacramentals, prayer, and saints, but there is a dire lack of help from a scriptural perspective.

Steeping you in scripture is the drive behind my whole ministry, every Bible study I write, every conference talk I offer, every Mass I participate in, and every radio show I produce, and it's why I cling to the sacraments and work hard at keeping my heart and life as pure as I can: so I can be an effective instrument in the hands of the Holy Spirit in equipping the saints in the Word of God for their works of ministry (Eph 4:12). Scripture is the banister you grab for when feeling around the dark cellar stair of fear.

The scriptures are the sharp, two-edged sword that proceeds from Jesus' mouth (Rv 1:16) and defeats the lawless one (2 Thes 2:8). This is the weapon he used when tempted by Satan in the desert, and he teaches us how to use it there.

Soldiers in training learn to make their weapon an extension of the body. They eat and sleep with it. They learn how to sharpen it, draw it, and use it to inflict a mortal wound. If my weapon fails because I failed to keep it clean and sharp or I did not use it properly, I die. Wielding a sword is something that takes time and practice. Gladiators must practice handling it properly, familiarizing themselves with the weight and dexterity of it, and learning which moves work best when, whether offensive or defensive.

However, note that the sword is sheathed in the belt of truth. Satan knows scripture too and uses it to deceive us (Mt 4). Unless your sword is grounded or sheathed in the truth, meaning interpreted properly, it is useless in either offense or defense against the enemy. This is especially important in matters of spiritual warfare, when scripture is a principal weapon and a lack of proper authority can yield tragic consequences.

The Sword Is Sheathed in the Church

Interpretation of scripture is never an individual matter: "First of all you must understand this, that no prophecy of scripture is a matter of one's own interpretation" (2 Pt 1:20). All scripture is prophecy because it all witnesses to Christ (Rv 19:10). If there is no private interpretation, the interpretation is public.

"Public" does not mean we are prohibited or discouraged from reading and understanding the Bible for ourselves. The Catholic Church does not tell us what to believe, holding the Faith over our heads like a mallet. She simply tells us what is worthy of belief, holding faith up to the light like a prism, so that its entire spectrum of color can illuminate the human race as Jesus intended.

"Public interpretation" means when we read and study scripture we must do so within the living tradition of the whole historical Church. All of us—past, present, and future—are under "one Lord, one faith, one baptism" (Eph 4:5). The Bible is the most mysterious and difficult book ever written and ever published. Since abuse of or mishandling even the most powerful weapon can lead to accidental death, should we not approach our study of the Word of God with a respect for the Christians of history, especially those who lived, wrote, and were martyred closest to the apostles and indeed were directly taught and ordained by them? Our ancient tradition helps protect us from error and is a rich source of teaching, knowledge, and blessing.

As a former non-Catholic I experienced firsthand the confusion inherent in separating biblical interpretation from Church history. For instance, my former denomination taught that salvation is a single point in time in which you pray particular words and is permanent from that point of time forward, no matter what sin you may commit afterward.

Yet, my study of the scriptures revealed that salvation is spoken of throughout the Bible in three ways: as occurring in the past, present, and future. Greek verbs confirm the forward "motion" of "being saved." Furthermore, Jesus never used such a formula when drawing people to himself. He never said, "Ask me into your heart and you'll be saved. Forever. No matter what."

In fact, he said the opposite, many, many times. Here are two instances: "No one who puts his hand to the plow and looks back is fit for the kingdom of God" (Lk 9:62), and "Every tree that does not bear good fruit is cut down and thrown into the fire" (Mt 7:19–20). What a relief to find the balanced, historical interpretation of absolute confidence in our salvation without the disrespectful presumption on God's grace! Salvation cannot be "lost" like a nickel dropped from one's pocket, but it most certainly can be forfeited, as both the Bible and the historical Church have always taught.

Additionally, I have known men and women of deep, lively faith who vehemently disagreed on the interpretation of scripture on points that are necessary to salvation: Baptism and the Eucharist, for instance. Is Baptism salvific or not? Is the Eucharist ordinarily necessary for salvation as the Bible says? Shouldn't we know? Wouldn't Jesus take great pains to make sure we know the unequivocal truth about things so foundational and eternally important?

The Holy Spirit is the very air the Church breathes in order to stay alive, "the Spirit of Truth" who "will guide you into all the truth" (Jn 16:13). He is not schizophrenic, he is not confused, and he would not tell me one thing and another Christian or a whole denomination of his Body something else entirely. So where is the truth?

"The pillar and foundation of truth" St. Paul describes is not my bible, and it is not my experiences in prayer, my private revelation, or my opinions (1 Tm 3:15, NABRE). This pillar and foundation is the *Church*. The Church is my measuring stick when discerning what the Bible means and how to apply it. The Church only authoritatively speaks on few passages of scripture.

When she does interpret, though, what the Church says on an issue is what the Holy Spirit says about it.

By "Church" I don't mean one person in the Church; I mean the Deposit of Faith as handed down to us through the last two thousand years by the successors of the apostles. I can obey the Church, and therefore obey God, but if I disobey the Church, I have disobeyed God himself. "Let every person be subject to the governing authorities; for there is no authority except from God, and those that exist have been instituted by God. Therefore whoever resists authorities resists what God has appointed, and those who resist will incur judgment" (Rom 13:1–2).

Contraception is a perfect example of a difficult issue on which the Bible is virtually silent but the Church has taught definitively since the apostles.[7] Apart from the living teaching authority of the Catholic Church, I am easily led into error by the enemy. Scripture, itself, is clear on this: St. Paul repeats often that we are to pay attention to both the sacred oral word (called tradition by the Church) and the sacred written word (scripture) faithfully passed down to us (1 Thes 2:13; 2 Thes 2:15, 3:6; and 2 Tm 2:2 are a few examples).

We must study and read scripture with the Church throughout history in order stay united to the Holy Spirit by whom the scriptures were written and through whom they are applied today. Within the Church, I can hear God speak through the scriptures. The prayer of the Church also assists me in fearless spiritual warfare, particularly through the Mass and sacraments, especially the Eucharist and the counsel of Confession, also called the sacrament of humility.

I function in relationship to the Church, so I can hear God speak in, with, and through the Church. Remember that exorcists say that during exorcism demons behave in ways that show they are defined and bound by the Catholic religious system, including its authority and interpretations. In the Church rests the full authority of God on earth so that the gates of hell will not prevail against it (Mt 16:18–19). In the context of the Church, I have the full armor of God.

Proper interpretation and context sharpens the two-edged sword and brings it into a position of perfect balance; it is then able to pierce between the soul and spirit (Heb 4:12). This truth is absolute, unalloyed and without the slightest bend, so that anything that does not conform to it breaks upon it and feels its invincible and immutable justice. Do your homework and hone your blade on the bedrock of truth, and you will do great damage to the kingdom of darkness.

Ultimately, though, it is imperative to remember that the armor, the sword, and the battle are all God's: "That all this assembly may know that the LORD saves not with [literal] sword and spear; for the battle is the LORD's and he will give you into our hand" (1 Sm 17:47). In all this talk of battles and warfare, what we're really doing is advancing behind shields of faith beside our neighbor in the armor of God and peeking out to hurl scripture bombs at the enemy.

Praying Always

The last encouragement St. Paul offers as we stand firm in our armor is prayer: "Pray at all times in the Spirit, with all prayer and supplication. To that end keep alert with all perseverance, making supplication for all the saints" (Eph 6:18).

Prayer gives me access to the full arsenal of heaven, and yet it is the simplest of practices and possibly the most mysterious of spiritual disciplines. As "easily difficult" as coffee with an invisible friend, prayer is also as multifaceted and mystifying as any journey in the universe. Indeed, our entire lives can and should be prayer: "pray without ceasing" (1 Thes 5:17, DRB).

Through prayer, we tap into the power and imagination that created the cosmos. Prayer gives permission for heaven to invade earth, the domain of human decisions and free will, on our behalf. In prayer we plumb the depths of the Spirit, conquer old enemies, and navigate new spiritual terrain.

The Church Triumphant, the full power of all the angels and saints, is ever standing by to help us in battle (Heb 12:1). Among the prayers we can offer and the saints we can petition in spiritual warfare must be the Rosary; the St. Michael Prayer; St. Joseph, the terror of demons; and St. Dymphna, the patron of those with anxiety and depression. Our guardian angels stand by. Mass is prayer. Adoration is prayer. Lectio divina is prayer. Working in our vocation is prayer. Fasting is prayer. Almsgiving is prayer. There are too many useful writings, saints, hymns, and prayers to name here, and a comprehensive list of those is not the purpose of this book.[8]

Instead, obedience is prayer, Fr. Jean-Pierre de Caussade, St. Francis de Sales, and St. Teresa of Calcutta, tell us. "Don't look for big things . . . just do small things with great love. The smaller the thing, the greater must be our love."[9] Just obey and pray, and pray without ceasing, as an individual and in community. Pray the scriptures, especially the ones in this book. Make your prayers the punctuation marks of your day. If you don't know what to pray about, observe what the enemy is doing and pray the opposite.

There's a big conversation going on in heaven. When he knows I am present in my armor and ready to pray, God will let me in on that big conversation. And in doing so, he will conform me to my "is-ness." He will download his strategies into my heart and life, and I will begin taking massive ground for his kingdom. He will teach me to be transparent; I will surrender former allegiances and abandon myself to love.

Let's Review

- *I have no armor of my own against the enemy.*

- *Without God I can do nothing* (Jn 15:5).

- *The armor and sword of the Word that God gives me are his.*

- *The Bible never calls me to fight* on offense against the devil. I am only commanded to resist the devil and stand firm in the armor of God.

- *The truth calls me to "gird my loins"* and makes me battle ready.

- *The Gospel peace of God makes me fearless* and gives me sure footing.

- My own righteousness is "as filthy rags" (Is 64:6, NKJV), but *Jesus has given me his righteousness to protect my heart within his forever.*

- *Acting on what God says in his Word quenches the fiery darts* of the enemy.

- *Trusting in my position in Christ by virtue of the sacraments guards my thoughts* against the lies of Satan.

- *My offensive weapon in spiritual warfare is the Word* of God in the scriptures and the Church.

- *"No weapon that is fashioned against you shall prosper,* and you shall confute every tongue that rises against you in judgment. This is the heritage of the servants of the LORD and their vindication from me, says the LORD" (Is 54:17), when you wear the armor of God and wield his unworldly weapon, the sword of the Word.

An Invitation

As we saw, the last thing St. Paul tells us regarding our armor is to "pray at all times in the Spirit, with all prayer and supplication. To that end keep alert with all perseverance" (Eph 6:18). If you have been marking important scriptures as you go, participating in the Invitation and God Prompt sections, and applying the scriptures in *Fearless* to your life, you have been following St. Paul's instruction by praying the scriptures with me.

Even so, in order to make steady progress from fear to love, one must immerse oneself in the scriptures on a daily basis, for at least a few minutes every day. *There is no better way* to hear him speak to us specifically and personally about our lives and fears. "All Scripture is inspired by God and profitable for teaching, for reproof, for correction, and for training in righteousness" (2 Tm 3:16). "Ignorance of the scriptures is ignorance of Christ," said St. Jerome.[10]

We read and study in order to experience God's voice and movement in our lives; as the mystic St. Bernard says so poetically: "The person who thirsts for God eagerly studies and meditates on the inspired Word, knowing that there, he is certain to find the One for whom he thirsts."[11] Nothing is more thrilling than walking with God. Sincerely seeking God's face in the scriptures on a daily basis will revolutionize your life.

No doubt you have heard the Word of God proclaimed at Mass or read snippets online or in books or magazines. But have you ever taken it up to read, allowing each word to penetrate your heart until you could hear the very voice of God speaking to you as clearly as I am speaking to you now?

Jesus challenged "religious" people who go through the motions without ever attending to the voice of the Spirit, saying, "Have you never read in the Scriptures?" (Mt 21:42).

So many Catholics listen to the readings every week, or even every day, at Mass but never stop to consider the liberating power of the Word of God in their lives, or that God is—daily and personally—speaking directly to them there. That so many have never experienced the mysterious encounter with the divine Other waiting for them in the scriptures is utterly tragic to me, and I have devoted my life to helping reverse that reality.

Diving deep into scripture is the only way to become truly fearless in our understanding of who God is and what he wants for us and from us. The sacraments are powerful sources of strength and healing, but they are only half the equation:

> The Church has always venerated the Scriptures as she venerates the Lord's Body. She never ceases to present to the faithful the bread of life, taken from *the one table of God's Word and Christ's Body*. In Sacred Scripture, the Church constantly finds her nourishment and her strength, for she welcomes it not as a human word, but as what it really is, the word of God. In the sacred books, the Father who is in heaven comes lovingly to meet his children, and talks with them. (CCC, 103–4, emphasis added)

Part of the "one table" of the Lord, the Word of God offers the objective self-knowledge and understanding that are absolutely necessary to becoming truly fearless Christians in a world careening in diversions and confused unreality. We must let the sap of the Holy Spirit animate our religious practice to truly love well, and that happens particularly in the Bible.

That means being in the Bible every day, memorizing God's Word, and knowing and understanding the scriptures. By becoming familiar with the Word of God, you are storing away spiritual weapons for the Spirit to use. He never fails to bring to your mind those passages that apply to the situation you are facing. Your mind will be trained to think as God thinks. You will be able to pierce through the lies and deceptions of the enemy. You will maintain focus amid the onslaught of distractions in the world around you.

I hope you will find a systematic schedule for exploring the Bible that works for you and stick to it. Start small, maybe only fifteen minutes. I pray you will especially consider the daily readings from the lectionary (the Church's daily scripture schedule of readings, available online or sometimes through your parish bulletin), or subscribe to a daily print resource such as *Magnificat* or an online resource such as Usccb.org or ApostleshipofPrayer.org.

Reading and studying scripture is more than an individual expression, because it also happens in and with the global Church. It's a community endeavor (Acts 2:42–47). Reading and studying scripture is both an individual expression of love and trust for God and a communal expression of our faith. How can our hearts be converted to the will of God if we force the Word of God to convert to a personal agenda? The simple answer is, they can't.

This is especially true of scripture *study*, when we primarily want to know what the scriptures *mean*. Participating in a Catholic Bible study, six to eight weeks or so, in spring *and* fall is a good practice, but at least once a year is important. Online is fine and convenient, but with a group is better.

Please, and I am pleading, use only Catholic Bible studies and resources. We must study and read the scriptures with the Church throughout history in order stay united to the Holy Spirit by whom they were written.

In order to read the scriptures on a daily basis with the Church, I use the Divine Office, the texts that the whole Church prays, offers, and prescribes. I adjust my practice and spirit to that, so that the Office gets me out of myself and into the flow of what the Holy Spirit is already achieving in the Church, which he has been building and nurturing for millennia.

The passages I read each day are being read all over the world, particularly the Mass readings. I am convinced the Holy Spirit saved a huge thrill for me when showing me the Office for the first time, by pointing out how my circumstances and his voice were addressed by the readings of the day, readings chosen hundreds of years before and that the global Church prays on any given day. I can know I am in the flow of what the Holy Spirit is doing by reading the daily readings of the Church, and it's not a matter of chance at all.

Currently, my practice is to read the whole Divine Office of readings for the day—morning, Mass, and evening readings—altogether, in the morning after my Rosary. the Rosary, the Office, including a meditation with the Church Fathers, and some time spent listening and contemplating takes about one hour. You may not have time for that, and that's fine. Simply read and pray over the Gospel reading for the day. For just the Gospel,

I love the *Pray as You Go* podcast on my Laudate app or online.

But before you do it, and every time you open the scriptures or hear them read out loud (at church), ask the Holy Spirit what he wants to say to you, and always expect him to speak. Do this every day, Dear One, and I promise you the Holy Spirit will begin unleashing a fearlessness in your heart and life in wonderful ways you could never guess. Let's practice.

God Prompt

Possibly my favorite thing about what I do is the special gifts God seems to have waiting for me in you. This past year I was welcomed into the bosom of a women's group in Minnesota and spoke at their retreat. On Sunday of that weekend, we all received copies of *Using the Sword of the Spirit*—a handy book of scriptures arranged topically as a go-to in times when we need verses pertaining to a specific issue. As talk of spiritual warfare ensued, one of the participants shared a daily callisthenic ritual she does as part of her morning prayer and offering that I never forgot. Maybe you'll want to try doing this every day for a week and see what surprising thing God does. How about standing up right now and trying it with me?[12] Betty does it like this:

- *Stand up with your arms stretched out to your sides, look up, and imagine the armor falling onto you piece by piece:* clink . . . clink . . . clink!

- *Make wide circles around your waist, front to back and say,* "Stand ready, with truth as a belt tight around your waist." (The truth is I am a child of God! He made me. I belong to him. I am his.)

- *Cross your arms over your chest as if you're receiving a blessing at Communion and say,* "With righteousness as your breastplate."

- *With palms up, extend your arms downward toward your feet and say,* "And as your shoes the readiness to announce the Good News of peace."

- *Turn around in a circle and say,* "At all times carry faith as a shield; for with it you will be able to put out all the burning arrows shot by the Evil One."

- *Put your arms over your head to make a hat and say,* "Accept salvation as a helmet."

- *Lift one arm as if you're brandishing a sword and say,* "And the Word of God as the sword which the Spirit gives you."

- *Make prayerful hands and say,* "Do all this in prayer, asking for God's help. Pray on every occasion, as the Spirit leads. For this reason keep alert and never give up; pray always for all God's people" (Eph 6:14–18, GNT).

- Lastly, say the Our Father, the Hail Mary, and the Glory Be.

7

*F*earless Transparency

Surrendering Allegiances

Few things are as overwhelming to me as the paint counter at the local hardware store. Just when you've found that perfect shade of white you discover another hundred you hadn't even considered. They all look white until you compare them to one another, or to black. Compared to black you can really pick up on the subtle differences in tone and shade.

Like those paint chips, sometimes to get the clearest possible picture of something, one must look at its opposite. In a sort of disciple Oreo sandwich, we're going to compare three mini-portraits by examining their allegiances: two instances in which Jesus directly attributed someone's behavior to Satan, and one other in the middle to contrast.

We've already discovered that the proper name Satan means *opponent* or *adversary* and is from the root meaning to *withstand*, *resist*, *cramp*, *bind*, or *attack*. Like the terms The Pill, Hooters, Ragu, or Catholic, originally the term *satan* was simply a noun; later it became a proper name. Any enemy or thing that stood in one's way was a satan.

Maybe that's why the winds of treachery have begun gusting around Jesus with increasing intensity.

Jesus Interrupted

For a time, the religious authorities were too absorbed with their self-serving political schemes to bother with the Galilean prophet, but their animosity has multiplied as quickly as the loaves and fishes.

Parallel passages provide the backdrop of a quiet moment. Jesus and his disciples have left the village and wandered along the forest country at the foot of the gray-haired Mt. Hermon cluster, where the snowmelt feeds the first springs of the Jordan and a cathedral of pines beckons Jesus to pray with them under their silent, uplifted arms.

Jesus is interrupted. Making use of the opportunity, or perhaps attempting to discern the timing of rapidly approaching events, he poses to the disciples the question of his identity and popular conclusions about it (Lk 9:18). Their disappointed answer is that he is some prophet or other but not the awaited Messiah.

They say it as if they want Jesus to remove their doubt. Although a handful of glittering marvels proclaimed him so, they lit up the spiritual night like fireworks: a shooting flare, a brilliant shower of color, and then a recovering, silent gloom while an ember glows wherever it has fallen. Throughout the Promised Land these three years, Light shone in the darkness, "and the darkness did not comprehend it" (Jn 1:5, DRB).

Jesus redirects, "And now for your part. What is the truth about me?"

Ever Ancient, Ever New

The strength of Peter's faith, quick and lively as of old, drew away the curtain concealing the Savior's divinity with the drama of a theater's grand drape. "You are the Christ, the Son of the living God" (Mt 16:16).

Did they all gasp at hearing it spoken aloud? Did the earth shiver as the warm, welcome proclamation of truth reverberated over its cold bones? Only the third person of the Holy Trinity could have made Peter sure enough for his mouth to open so the words could fly.

With his statement, Peter reached the pinnacle. No other Petrine moment in the scriptures reaches the height of this one. He is publicly blessed, publicly anointed, publicly installed and positioned, and publicly elevated with the authority of Christ himself. In the footsteps of Old Testament Joseph (Gn 41:40–44) and Eliakim (Is 22:20–23), he is made second only to the King, given the keys to the kingdom, the robe, the ring, the protection, the authority, and the service. The Church, the Body of Christ himself, will take shape over Peter and be supported by his priestly office. Such authority can only be divinely given, and it was; Jesus promised.

Still, straight before Jesus there stretches a weary way of sorrows, and right away, as though there is no time to lose, he begins to reveal what being the Christ really means. Although he does not go so far as to specify the brutal violence and humiliation of a Roman crucifixion, he begins to prepare them for the near eventualities that will shortly challenge his divinity by speaking openly about his death for the first time.

The Adversary

For Peter, who was basking in anticipation, praise, and joy, immanent death—any death, but especially the death of the Son of God—must have been unimaginable. How is it even possible? Why should it be so? Peter pulls Jesus aside in painful rebuke and begs him to spare himself and all the rest of them.

Was Peter motivated by love, even if perhaps puffed up with some importance? Was he ignorant of the awful implications of all Jesus was revealing and simply babbling nervously through it? Or was something else involved, something all the disciples suddenly shared as deeply as they shared in Peter's earlier confession? What if they heard and understood every detail of what Jesus was conveying? What if they were *terrified of losing him?*

And with an all-seeing eye toward the listening disciples, Jesus speaks in a tone so loud that those who heard Peter's tribute might also witness his correction: "Get behind me, Satan! You are a *hindrance* to me; for you are not on the side of God, but of men" (Mt 16:23, emphasis added).

Ignorant as the stumble probably was, Peter had ceased following Christ and begun attempting to lead him. Jesus might as well have said, "You are a satan! Your allegiance is to security." Peter was thwarting Jesus' purpose *out of fear*; Peter's fear had become a *trap* for Jesus (*hindrance* meaning *trap*); and like Satan, he had set himself up against God as one who blindly gropes in darkness because he cannot comprehend the light of humility, the life in redemptive suffering. Dear One, is your fear an invisible, spiritual trap for someone you love, perhaps a child or a spouse?

Satan found a foothold in Peter's fear, and however unknowingly or innocently, Peter attended to Satan's suggestion to interrupt the will of God, to oppose Jesus' glory, the redemption of humankind, and the destruction of the devil's kingdom, just as Satan had done the first time all the humility of the Incarnation was revealed to him.

And it was the night before Christ suffered, when Peter would go from arguing over his greatness to deserting his King, that Jesus warned Peter, "Simon, Simon, behold, Satan demanded to have you, that he might sift you like wheat, but I have prayed for you that your faith may not fail" (Lk 22:31–32).

From Rock to Rubble

The conversation between Jesus and Satan implied in Jesus' statement is reminiscent of the permission Satan obtained from God to test Job that we'll talk about in the DVD for this chapter. Satan "demanded" or "desired" Peter. What a foreboding statement. Isn't the trepidation made more so with the knowledge that Jesus saw it ahead of time and, rather than preventing it, prayed for Peter's strengthening after his failure? Under Jesus' penetrating eye, the rock will crumble, reduced to a pebble.

What could account for so great a defection from so dedicated a disciple? Satan will "sift" Peter, and he will use his fear to do it, the fear Satan saw on display in his rebuke of Christ. The word *sift* means to examine closely or to separate what is rough from what is fine. Satan wants to thresh Peter's faith, to beat the small, hard kernel of it until it's broken open and exposed to the cold eyes of the world and, more clearly, to Peter himself. Satan wants him destroyed; Jesus wants him purified in preparation for his ministry.

The Message in the Emotion

Jesus rebuked the disciples' fear repeatedly, but it wasn't the emotion itself that Jesus reacted so strongly to. After all, fear and all our emotions are part of a normal, healthy life, and they don't exist in a vacuum; they are influenced by our physical health and rest, or lack thereof; by our thought patterns; and by our spiritual input. I am not in any way advocating that we disregard or deny fear or any other emotion, and neither is Jesus. Fear, in itself, is not bad.

Instead, remember that emotions are the voice of relationships. They function like Doppler radar, constantly updating us on the status of our relationships. They know when there's a storm coming. But sometimes they result from too much or too little input. Think about how you feel when watching a particular thriller movie. None of it is real at all, but your body and emotions react to the unreality, what they see and hear, as though it is. Our emotions were not intended to rule us; disordered passions are a result of the Fall.

Emotions have a mental component, so they follow from what we think: what I think about a situation is how I will react to it. When we react emotionally as though we have no facts to guide our decisions, we are "like a wave of the sea that is driven and tossed by the wind" (Jas 1:6).

Emotions were not designed, nor were they ever intended, to be the basis for our actions. Actions are meant to be determined by God's absolute truth. Action begins in my mind. Feelings add color and vibrancy to our lives, but they should never be solely in charge. Dark emotions, including fear, add to the richness of emotional expression designed by our Creator and are useful in alerting us to real danger. But no emotion should dominate or control us. When dark emotions continually envelop us, we should consider ourselves spiritually sidetracked.[1]

When we internalize God's Word and use it as the foundation for our behavior, we can choose our actions. Jesus told the disciples he would be killed but that he would rise again. Did they understand completely what "rising again" meant? They probably did not, but should they have *believed* him when he said it? You bet. "Why are *you* terrified, O you of little faith?" (Mt 8:26, NABRE, emphasis added).

Jesus was confronting the disciples' fear of suffering. He was challenging their fear of the death of someone they loved; they had no idea, yet, of their own suffering where he was concerned. And neither do we.

The ones we love will suffer. They will. We often forget how pervasive and insistent, and sometimes excruciating, the Fall is. But be at peace; Jesus knows: "I have said this to you, that in me you may have peace. In the world you have tribulation; but be of good cheer, I have overcome the world" (Jn 16:33). "Therefore do not be anxious about tomorrow, for tomorrow will be anxious for itself. Let the day's own trouble be sufficient for the day" (Mt 6:34). Today's trouble is plenty; don't you think? St. Mary Magdalene shows us how to turn our fear for someone we love into the power of faith.

The Prophetess

Betrayal is in the air; Jesus' hour has come. The turning point was raising Lazarus from the dead, and the opposition is frenzied. Here at Mary, Martha, and Lazarus's house in Bethany there is an eye of peace in the cyclone.

If you knew you had only six days to live, how would you spend that time? In his last days on earth Jesus is at a dinner party in the shelter of close friends. Lazarus's shocking resurrection from the dead makes him the center of conversation and speculation. There are occasional surreptitious glances cast Jesus' way. Who *does* such things? What will he do next?

Where are Jesus' reflections as he listens to the celebration in Lazarus's home with his sisters, Mary and Martha; the disciples; and the townsfolk of Bethany— enjoying the hospitality, the meal, the conversation? Is it already a shroud of isolation over his every action and thought, this lonely knowledge of impending terror?

Perhaps it is because Mary senses something mournful in him that she rises amid the bustle and chatter, unveiling to her Lord first her hair and then her soul, in perfect transparency for the whole company to witness. The room grows as silent as her tears when the former prostitute stands and uncovers her hair. Every eye, every opinion, is trained on her.

In shameless vulnerability and scandalous display of impromptu devotion, she kneels to break open an alabaster box, pours an extravagant pound of essential oil on divine feet fresh from grimy gospel roads, and performs a slave's duty by cleaning Jesus' feet. And as if she could not possibly debase herself enough there on the floor, she uses her long, dark, uncovered hair to blot them. The silence is fleeting, for her breach of etiquette and position as a woman in the culture makes her magnificent self-donation and generosity the center of scandal and a supreme embarrassment.

All of the disciples have been told, now, what is imminent, but their preconceptions of Jesus' reign and visions of personal grandeur prevent their understanding him. The Gospels of Matthew and Mark reveal that the disciples are offended by Mary's display, thinking it inappropriate and bold, even proud. Sharply critical, it is Judas who gives voice to their murmuring and rebukes her wastefulness, contributing to the exorbitant cost of the ointment in her precious box.

How the insult must have hurt. The light is shining, but the darkness cannot "comprehend" it (Jn 1:5, DRB). Literally, *comprehend* means "to wrap one's mind around" or to "ambush" it. Humility throws utter confusion into the enemy camp.

More Precious Than Diamonds

A former staff member of the Catholic Worker tells the story of a woman who donated a diamond ring.[2] Later Dorothy Day gave it to a crazy homeless woman, leading someone to say, "Wouldn't it have been better if we had sold that ring and paid the woman's rent for a year?"

Dorothy replied that the woman had her dignity and could do what she liked with it. She could sell it for rent money or take a trip to Hawaii. Or she could enjoy wearing a diamond ring on her hand like the woman who gave it away. "Do you suppose God created diamonds only for the rich?"

The notorious Judas, a lover of money who steals from the common purse, would certainly never similarly "waste" an item of such value when it should secretly line his own pocket. Indignant over Mary's indulgence as she bathes the body of Christ in an elaborate sacrifice of praise, Judas proves that he who is forgiven little loves little (Lk 7:47), for his next recorded act is to sell the Savior to his executioners (Mt 26:14).

In thanksgiving for the resurrection of Lazarus, the family has served Jesus a feast, a gift, but of the gifts he received that night, it is doubtful that any was as poignant and significant to Jesus as that alabaster box of oil.

Oil is a potent scriptural symbol of the Holy Spirit, as our sacrament of Confirmation illustrates. Although carefully preserved for this most special occasion and poured from the hand of a former prostitute possessed by demons, it was the Holy Spirit then, through Mary Magdalene, who anointed Christ for death and burial, fulfilling in a literal way the Old Testament title *Christ*, meaning "anointed one." Pope Benedict said of her gift, "There is only one anointing that is strong enough to meet death, and that is the anointing of the Holy Spirit, the love of God."[3]

Mary Magdalene was arguably the disciple most savaged by the misery of sin, living unmarried in a man's world, and was therefore most vulnerable, especially to their criticism and derision as fellow disciples. And yet her allegiance was to Jesus. She surrendered to his death. She was *fearless* in her love for him.

Mary's risking complete transparency moved him deeply; he took a public stand for and memorialized her, and Dear One, when Jesus defends you, you have been *defended*.

Although it occurred in the presence of all those at the celebratory dinner, it was a private moment, for while the disciples were untouched by and oblivious to the fragrance of worship filling the house that night

(Jn 12:4), Jesus *saw into* her gift to him. He gathered it up and tossed it into the future, into our laps this very moment, suggesting we reevaluate where wastefulness really lies. How wasteful is stinginess? The third person of the Trinity was preparing Jesus for impending death, and he used this spontaneous, simple, heartfelt display of love to do what was prophetic and divine, a significance indiscernible by anyone but Jesus.

Dare I say Jesus *needed* what she gave that night? Is it blasphemous to suggest he may have felt alone, isolated, and misunderstood and therefore needed affirmation? Could her show of love have strengthened him? And if it is possible that Jesus needed human affirmation of love from those he served, I don't have to be ashamed that I need it.

Mingled with tears and prophetic insight, the scented oil becomes potent enough behind the ears of each millennium for the fragrance to linger to this day, proving that no amount of love, praise, or transparency can be wasted on him; it's only ever multiplied.

On the Cross, he would be stripped of everything but the scented oil that Mary had poured out of the veins of her broken alabaster box. And when his unblemished body was broken, his blood spilling out onto a rotten, smelly, dusty earth—from whip, thorn, nail, and chalice—the balm of his transparent love would scent and save and heal all of history.

A woman's hair is her glory, the scriptures say (1 Cor 11:15, DRB), and so Mary, always at the feet of Jesus, wiped his tired and dirty feet with her glory, placing the noblest part of her body beneath his feet and approaching him not as a mere man, St. Chrysostom says, but as God.[4] She lowered herself as low as she could go, and her humility was powerful enough to go with Jesus to the Cross and the grave.

Satan tells us we have to "be strong" and to fight
for our rights. He tries to make us think we have to take
what we need or want, when what's really true is that
we have to give it *all*, and that's where the power is.
There is no greater spiritual authority than to go low,
to let "them" have the last say, and to take second, or
even last, place.

It was Mary's fierce transparency and sacrifice *in the
face of her fear* that touched Jesus so deeply, proceeding
from a love and a glory centered in him. Obedient to the
prompting of the Holy Spirit, she anticipated his death
and, unlike Peter, fearlessly helped prepare him for it.
In risking absolute transparency, she was the prophetic
instrument used to anoint the Son for the grave. Of all
the people present, Mary and Jesus were the only two
in the house that night who smelled the fragrance of
that oil.

The Devil

Judas Iscariot. The infamous betrayer. The activist, some
say. Doesn't just seeing the name make you shudder?
We all know and have been victims of a Judas. She's a
BFF, or even family, maybe a sister, but she's two-faced. I
find she has exposed my vulnerabilities, told my secrets,
ridiculed what is priceless to me, and mocked me to
my friends. She has stabbed me in the back while keeping her loyal facade smilingly in place. Hard to find is
loyalty.

The psalmist relates a similar experience: "It is
not an enemy who taunts me—then I could bear it; it
is not an adversary who deals insolently with me—
then I could hide from him. But it is you, my equal, my
companion, my familiar friend. We used to hold sweet

converse together; within God's house we walked in fellowship" (Ps 55:12–14).

He must have been an influential disciple; he was the treasurer who held the purse strings and reclined in a place of some intimacy and position at Jesus' side, opposite John, at the last Passover table. He was so near that Jesus was able to dip his bread in the dish and feed it to Judas as a sign of his falseness.

Hard to imagine he walked in Jesus' tired footsteps for three years, heard the power of God leap from his lips, watched him exhaust himself in healing and restoring the mobs, and saw him call forth Lazarus from the dead. How did he witness it all and not desire Jesus himself? Judas let Jesus wash his feet and accepted the Eucharist from his hand while having already sold him for a mere tenth of what he complained Mary's spikenard was worth.

Like Peter, Judas's allegiance was also to security, but for him safety lay in money. The Bible tells us Judas skimmed off the top of the treasury; he's a lover of money, greedy, a thief who embezzles from even a nonprofit. He's touchy, easily offended, and provoked to revenge by what he cannot believe or understand (Jn 6:66–70). He is judgmental and hypocritical too, since it was Judas who was offended by and instigated the accusation of wastefulness against Mary (Jn 12:4–6).

Matthew tells us Judas was not simply an opportunist; he *sought out* the chief priests right after Jesus' correction in Bethany and offered to betray him for a bribe. Then he waited for the right moment to hand him over, away from the crowds (Mt 26:14–16).

Jesus knew of his duplicity, having forewarned Judas weeks ago when he took part in complaining over Jesus' mysterious teaching on the literal consumption of his Body and Blood as necessary for salvation. The early writings of the Church put forth that this was the point when Judas permanently silenced the struggle between his greed and his calling, the moment when he turned away from Christ in his heart: "Did I not choose you, the Twelve, and one of you is a devil?" (Jn 6:70).

The statement in that question must have electrified the air. The term *devil* is *diabolos* in Greek, and means *accuser*, *slanderer*, or *Satan*. Jesus uses similar terms several times to speak of Judas. What does it mean? The Fathers believe it probably does not mean Judas was possessed, but we can speculate he was specially influenced by Satan. I wonder what it felt like to hear Jesus say this. Both Peter and Judas know.

Surely they all looked around, sizing one another up. Judas was the only one of the Twelve not from Galilee; he was an outsider. Did they suspect him? I bet Judas was made to know in his heart at that moment that Jesus spoke of him, that he chose Judas and kept him with full knowledge and consent all along.

Jesus had warned him, when he washed his feet, a hospitality ritual that symbolized the acceptance of a visitor and absence of any hostile intent by the host. He told Judas that his heart was impure, and yet he still took up the towel, poured water over his feet, and pressed callused heels between tender hands while Judas remained unmoved. "You are clean, but not every one of you" (Jn 13:10). But it's context, now, along with the thrill of gladness with which Jesus celebrates his last Passover with his band of brothers and the excess of love with which he offers them his Body and Blood as a leaving gift.

This entire "code" of hospitality in the Middle East was so strong that it was considered a grave insult, a mark of hostility, and even an act of war to refuse the refreshment of foot washing or a meal to guests. One of the most despicable acts in the ancient world was to eat with someone and then betray him.

In the Middle East, bread is used as an eating utensil. According to custom, the master of the feast put pieces of meat (lamb for Passover) onto a cupped bit of bread; dipped it into a dish of sauce, herbs (bitter herbs at Passover), or gravy; and placed it directly in the most honored guest's mouth. In fact, the host of a Middle Eastern meal today offers the honored bread in almost exactly the same hand-to-mouth way we are offered the Eucharist at Mass (so to refuse and stick one's hand out instead of receiving the bread on the tongue might be insulting to the Host).

Who is the betrayer, they all ask? No one suspects Judas, who says, "Is it I?" with them so that he, the false one, might remain hidden in the midst of them. Evil likes to hide in places where it's less conspicuous, where it won't be easily detected for the superficial mask of holiness and justice it wears: in the law and in the Church. Why are we surprised by a priest's scandal in the Church? How better to force and manipulate a person's will and scandalize and divide the Church, from Satan's point of view, than to use the trappings of holiness to deceive?

"This is my Body which will be given up for you." "He who has dipped his hand in the dish with me, will betray me" (Mt 26:23). In a dramatic moment that is both an unmasking of the traitor and a final plea in tender charity for repentance, Jesus refuses to treat Judas as the enemy he is, for he came to fulfill, not to destroy.

Instead he offers his Body to Judas as a close friend, the honored guest. Do their eyes meet in awkward realization, betrayer and betrayed? Does Judas sweat or flush, as the one who takes and eats unto sacrilege and becomes the first to be guilty of the Body and Blood of Christ (1 Cor 11:29)?

With the morsel of bread he blasphemed, Satan's grip was solidified in Judas's soul as he "entered into" Judas; and Jesus said, "What you are going to do, do quickly" (Jn 13:27). Judas went immediately forward to be lost to "perdition" within the blackness of everlasting gloom (Jn 17:12). What an awful tragedy. Satan could never have entered if Judas had not opened the place in his soul.

The Devil's Toys

Many guesses have been offered regarding why Judas betrayed Jesus, but like a detective attempts to understand a criminal's motives by discounting those that don't fit, only one of the suggestions has the clear ring of truth to me after all we've learned about Satan to this point.

True, Judas was habitually motivated by a love of money, and maybe that was the beginning of Satan's toehold in Judas's heart. But he only asked for thirty pieces of silver—about three month's wages—to hand Jesus over, and that he returned (Mt 27:1–5).

Agreed, he was a practical man, an account keeper; he was realistic, logical, opportunistic, and utilitarian. If Jesus was put to death, what would happen to the rest of the disciples, to him? When the tide of popularity turned, did Judas begin looking ahead and decide to take political precautions to protect himself? Was he simply jumping from a sinking ship by turning Jesus over?

I don't think so. The fact that he claimed in his own words to have betrayed "innocent blood," and hung himself once Jesus was arrested and condemned to death, says that Judas had no idea whatsoever that Jesus would actually be put to death (Mt 27:1–4) if he turned him in. So why would he betray Jesus if he didn't want him to die?

What if Judas didn't expect Jesus to die because he expected Jesus to fight? What if he was trying to force Jesus into a corner so he would use and show his full power? Imagine his excitement when Peter (finally!) drew a sword and cut off a soldier's ear. What despair must have engulfed Judas when Jesus told Peter to sheath his sword, restored the ear with a delicate touch, and delivered himself softly to the proud hour of darkness and death.

Here's the thing: Jesus' repeated allusions to a spiritual kingdom rather than a political one would have infuriated an Iscariot, who, it has been theorized, held membership in a group of Jewish political rebels intent on the overthrow of Roman occupation in Palestine. Such a spiritualized "kingdom" as Jesus preached must have seemed more idealistic and silly by the day.

The political upheaval in Palestine at the time was a pot near to boiling over. Jesus himself predicted the annihilation of Jerusalem within the generation (Mt 24), and indeed the Romans razed the city in AD 70. Judas surely hoped betraying him to the authorities would force Jesus' hand, and he would be pushed to assert his true power and begin the Jewish revolt that Judas longed for.

Jerusalem was full of pilgrims who would riot against Rome. The Jewish authorities knew it, so they contrived foisting Jesus' execution on the Romans because of his popularity. The Romans knew it, so Pilate gave the people the choice of a substitute in Barabbas. That Judas attempted to return the money to the authorities when Jesus was arrested, threw it in the Temple floor, and hung himself in despair afterward all suggest that he never anticipated Jesus would *not* fight for his life and freedom.

Judas wanted a war. Jesus was letting hookers touch him publicly and throw away funding for an uprising. When Jesus also refused to fight his arrest and execution, Judas's whole vision for what the Messiah was here to do must have collapsed. Could this be why the peoples' support also turned against Jesus so drastically after his arrest? Everyone was looking for a political Messiah! But Rome was not going to be conquered under Jesus; there was not going to be a revolution, at least not the way they imagined it.

In Judas we can discern what faith is, by looking at what it isn't. Peter surrendered his misdirected allegiance when Jesus called him to. Judas clung to what he hoped and expected Jesus would do. And now he's got nothing. Have you been here, Dear One?

Faith cannot simply be belief—in God, or in a set of teachings—for "even the demons believe—and shudder" (Jas 2:19). We go to church, pray, scold ourselves for wavering in second thoughts, and try to convince ourselves that we believe as much as is necessary for God to do what we think is right. If that fails, we attempt to force people and circumstances. But that's not faith. Great faith does not claim to know what only God can know; it claims only to know the God who knows.

Was Judas truly repentant or remorseful, or was he simply despondent that all his hopes for political salvation were empty? Why did Jesus say of him, "None of them is lost but the son of *perdition*, that the Scripture might be fulfilled," *perdition* meaning literally "son of *damnation*" (Jn 17:12; emphasis added)? One thing is sure, Judas was a trusted friend and apostle, but three years or more of entertaining greed and evil in his heart left him empty of love and willing to betray Jesus to those Judas himself hated. When force failed to gain the desired outcome and he realized his grave error, he had no allegiance to Jesus to fall back onto.

I don't know about you, but it's easy for me to feel sorry for Judas. I think the *Catechism* helps us here (CCC, 2090–92), because Judas seems to have suffered from despair and presumption: despair, because he ceased (if he ever had in the first place) looking to Jesus and hoped instead in earthly help and liberation in a Jewish nation and political system; presumption, because he believed by serving earthy efforts men were capable of freedom.

Like Satan from the beginning, Judas and most of the Jews of that time never got what Jesus was about. Judas could not get his head around the supreme power and authority of sacrifice and humility; like Mary's ointment, Jesus' whole ministry all seemed like so much waste if it wasn't used to social or political ends.

Rather than the long view of faith in who Jesus is, Judas had a short view; his faith was in what he thought Jesus should or would do. He attempted to force Jesus into his own construct, a man-made system of earthly power and authority, a government—with all the socio-economic trappings—that would "save" them all. Pope Benedict explains that

> at the heart of all temptations, as we see here, is the act of pushing God aside because we perceive him as secondary, if not actually superfluous and annoying, in comparison with all the apparently far more urgent matters that fill our lives.
>
> Constructing a world by our own lights, without reference to God, building on our own foundation; refusing to acknowledge the reality of anything beyond the political and material,

while setting God aside as an illusion—that is
the temptation that threatens us in many varied
forms.[5]

In succumbing to and maintaining allegiance to the
illusion, Judas was not unlike Peter who drew a sword
to fight and betrayed Jesus on the same night; the difference was that Peter surrendered to God's plan and
went out weeping over his betrayal in the face of such
sacrifice, whereas Judas followed Satan's attempts to
force and manipulate all the way to his self-execution
in the Valley of Hell (it was really called that). So goes
the saying: "All who take the sword will perish by the
sword" (Mt 26:52).

Black and White

Throughout *Fearless* we have been looking at the ways
Satan interacts with people and with God in order to
discern the hallmarks of his operation and influence
in our own fear, anxiety, and depression. Jesus directly
attributed Satan's activity to both Peter's and Judas's
actions, but ultimately Peter surrendered to God; Judas
did not.

Judas is proud. He forces and manipulates to get
his way, as though he knows what is good for others.
Judas incites division. He accuses Mary. He accuses
Jesus. He is unforgiving. He's ambitious. He's ruthless.
He is unsubmissive to God's plan. He wants what he
wants. Forget God's plan; I've got a plan: Let's conquer
Rome. Let's go people! Let's *do* this!

Judas's concern for the poor is fake, a false humility that is perhaps the most dangerously demonic.[6] His
relationship to Jesus and the apostles is sneaky. Judas

was with Jesus all that time but never softened by him. He watches Mary dump her oil, tears, and humility out on Jesus' feet, and all he has to say to her is, What. Are. You. *Doing*? Her holiness immediately provokes him to sell the Savior. He watches Jesus' arrest, seeing he will die a violent, innocent death, and all he can do is go out and hang himself because his little dream of a little coup is futile, not in God's plan after all. Wake *up*, Dear One!

I am proud. I am fake. I incite division in the church with my loud opinions and whispered gossip. I am unsubmissive to God's plan; just watch how I act when I don't get what I want. I am manipulative and critical. I judge others and find them *lacking*. Just give me what I want. I will not serve. I force my will on others and have to be first. It's my way or the highway. Geez, just get with the *program*, people!

When direct temptation failed to defeat the Messiah in the desert, he tried a subtler strategy. He worked his way into Jesus' heart and life through the ones he loved most. Don't be fooled into thinking that because he is divine Jesus was not deeply hurt by Judas's deceit and loss, even though he understood it better than anyone.

Knowing Judas a little better now, can you imagine how blessed Jesus felt receiving Mary's transparent, prophetic gesture? Look at the derision on Judas's face when he obtusely accuses her of wastefulness. See how low she stoops and how high Judas reaches. Look at her kiss Jesus' weary feet, while Judas kisses Jesus with betrayal on a cheek turned to him in peace.

Consider Mary and Judas's relationship to money.

Watch how they each relate to the disciples.

How does each react to God's plan in Christ, to Jesus himself, and to disillusionment?

Consider her oil and the Holy Spirit as a type of exorcism, in which Judas is expelled from the band of apostles by the strength of the humility he encountered.

Dear One, we should squash every single bit of pride we see in ourselves. We should throw it at Jesus' feet. Serve somebody. Whatever sin issue you struggle with deeply, find a way to humble it. The term *humble* comes from the root for *humus, soil,* meaning *close to the ground.* Humility is the soil in which all other virtues grow. Unanimously, the saints, the Church, and the Bible say humility is our greatest weapon in spiritual warfare. Through the humility of Christ, the devil was defeated.

I must clothe myself in the humility of truth and self-knowledge because our adversary is a roaring lion; I must remember that brandishing my strength fosters competition, but sharing my weakness fosters community; and I must acknowledge that I have nothing I was not first given. "What have you that you did not receive? If then you received it, why do you boast as if it were not a gift?" (1 Cor 4:7).

When direct attacks against trusting in God's timing, provision, or substance fail to affect you, Satan will move to subtler approaches. He will distract you. He will use the ones you love and who love you most to influence, oppose, and trap you in depression over the past and fear and anxiety for the future. You will fall every time if you are not aware of this reality, and if you don't anticipate this strategy, you will blame the person through whom the temptation comes, rather than the enemy behind him. We must always keep humbly in mind too that Eden teaches us that we women can be the first target and first influence for good or evil in others.

Defeating Disillusionment

At some point, even the most optimistic of us wrestles with disillusionment. Maybe the Christian who inspired you most betrayed you, sinned gravely, or left the Faith entirely. Perhaps you remember what the Church or the world used to be like and feel the faith and values of days gone by have been shoved aside for what barely looks like worship or decency at all. Possibly you prayed with all your heart, soul, mind, and strength for a miracle and God did not answer.

Or perhaps you believe your pastor is a jerk, an idiot, or a pervert. Maybe the direction of the Church, the pope, or the bishops seems adrift or awry. Are you looking around your empty nest or dreary cubicle wondering, *Is this all there is? Life is hard, and then you die? I thought there was supposed to be more.*

Every one of us, at some point, must face the fact that some cause we believed in completely—the one we gave our heart to, the party that had our confidence, or the venture we invested our lives or retirement in— some absolute truth that turned out to be not so true at all, and the throb of possibility we knew in our younger and more idealistic days have all taken on the cold edge of an unfulfilled and shockingly different reality, leaving us feeling as though faith has cheated and lied to us. What if it's *all* a grand lie?

How do I go on? What do I believe in? What do I do when I find myself struggling with the disorientation, disappointment, discouragement, disillusionment, and the whole tangle of fear, doubt, anxiety, anger, and depression that go with it?

Rejoice, Dear One!

Most people think disillusionment is negative; some equate it with cynicism. But having one's illusions ripped away—being dis-illusioned—is what Jesus meant when he said, "You will know the truth, and the truth will make you free" (Jn 8:32). Having an illusion removed, while painful, is necessary in any and all progress. Every stage of emotional, intellectual, and spiritual growth (remember that all growth is spiritual) *requires* this disillusionment. In order to accept or make room for anything new, one must clear a space and do away with the old.

If you are experiencing the grief of disillusionment, Beloved, be at peace. Nothing has gone horribly wrong. God is not jerking you around. He's shaking loose false ideas you have about him and about faith and life. Your false beliefs and expectations may be dying, and you may be experiencing the pain of that loss, but if you're honest, weren't your expectations somewhat unrealistic, illogical, emotion based, projected, or only partly founded in reality to begin with?

Psychology tells us depression is the natural process of letting go of something that is no longer useful. Maybe we're trapped in depression because of unforgiveness, which is attachment to an injury. Unforgiveness is especially dangerous because by refusing to forgive, we forfeit our own forgiveness (Mt 6:15). Depression, anxiety, and fear become deep and persistent when we continue to hang on to the offense long after we should have let go of the delusion. This is what happened to Judas. He would not surrender his allegiance to Jesus, and he despaired.

In scriptural terms, disillusionment is a necessity. The truth in the scriptures begins to strip away deceptions we weren't aware we cherished, and reality begins to dawn. Sometimes the truth is a fresh stream of living water on a parched spiritual landscape; sometimes it's an underlying agitation or vague feeling of dissatisfaction. But sometimes it's a blinding light that temporarily disorients, or an emotional earthquake that crumbles the foundations we stand on.

Like Judas, like Eve, like Mary, what we do next changes everything. That's why, throughout *Fearless*, we have probed what the scriptures say about evil and sin, so we actually "know the truth" and no longer buy the lies that keep us spiritually impotent. Otherwise we persist in depression, anxiety, and fear. Our intellects remain darkened, our wills stay weak, and our disordered appetites persist.

Archbishop Fulton Sheen said, "[Jesus] came to put a harlot above a Pharisee, a penitent robber above a high priest, and a prodigal son above his exemplary brother. To all the phonies and fakers who would say that they could not follow the pope or the Church because his Church was not holy enough, he would ask, 'How holy must the Church be before you will enter into it?'"[7]

So you were betrayed by a fellow Christian who exploited you or let you down? Are you alone in experiencing human hypocrisy? Is it smarter to harden your heart so you're never disappointed or betrayed again? That's what the Pharisees did, a hardness that paradoxically made them even more open to deception from the devil. That's what Judas did, and his intractable allegiances drove him to suicide.

A House Built on the Rock

Instead of armoring your heart, "consider him who endured from sinners such hostility against himself, so that you may not grow weary or fainthearted. In your struggle against sin you have not yet resisted to the point of shedding your blood" (Heb 12:3–4). We opine bitterly and weep pitifully as if we're the first who's ever been disappointed and disabused of Christian confetti and unicorns, as if Jesus' whole sordid betrayal, injustice, humiliation, and brutal murder never happened.

Doesn't disillusionment make me largely afraid of, depressed by, and anxious about ghosts? Is Jesus surprised by anything? The Church is founded on a Savior who endured all the nastiest, filthiest malice that fallen angels *and* humanity could contrive. And none of it shocks or disgusts him. He wades right into the sordidness of the human condition today, as prime potential, not problem.

It's I, like Judas—in my clamor for security and superiority, demand for bread and circuses, and misplaced allegiances—who lives in the illusion, not Jesus. And it is exactly those delusions that he, in his mercy, strips away when I am disillusioned.

So allow Jesus to disillusion you about just how evil and merciless people can be. Allow him to strengthen you for the real spiritual battle, the one he has already fought and won. Gird your loins and grow a pair and let's get busy ransacking our lives of sin and sloth with the sword of the scriptures so we can set the world on fire. In the Gospel of Matthew, we read,

> Every one then who hears these words of mine
> and does them will be like a wise man who built

> his house upon the rock; and the rain fell, and
> the floods came, and the winds blew and beat
> upon that house, but it did not fall, because it had
> been founded on the rock. And every one who
> hears these words of mine and does not do them
> will be like a foolish man who built his house
> upon the sand; and the rain fell, and the floods
> came, and the winds blew and beat against that
> house, and it fell; and great was the fall of it. (Mt
> 7:24–27)

Defeating disillusionment means getting our bearings and surrendering disillusionment to hope. Haven't you ever wondered why hope is one of the three theological virtues? It's because hope is divine; it must come from God if we're to have it at all in this world. Pray for hope, Dear One, when you feel hopeless, just as St. Paul does when he encourages us,

> We know that the whole creation has been groaning with labor pains together until now; and not only the creation, but we ourselves, who have the first fruits of the Spirit, groan inwardly as we wait for adoption as sons, the redemption of our bodies. For in this hope we were saved. Now hope that is seen is not hope. For who hopes for what he sees? But if we hope for what we do not see, we wait for it with patience." (Rom 8:22–25)

Hope's name is Jesus. To remain in hope, we keep our hearts and minds on him, knowing always that this world is not permanent.

That is why Paul tells us, "If then you have been raised with Christ, seek the things that are above, where Christ is, seated at the right hand of God. Set your minds on things that are above, not on things that are on earth"

(Col 3:1–2). Our God is a "God of hope" (Rom 15:13). Nothing can come between us and the love of Christ (Rom 8:38). Because of that hope, I can risk surrendering all my allegiances to Jesus and love extravagantly, even in the face of my disillusionment and fear.[8]

Let's Review

- *Satan tempts me to resist suffering that is part of God's plan,* both for my own life and for others'.

- *Emotions, like fear, are a natural part of a normal, healthy life.*

- *Satan capitalizes on my natural emotions,* by tempting me to allow them to overwhelm or control my behavior.

- *We can choose our actions* when we internalize God's Word and use it as the foundation for our behavior.

- *My most natural, simple gestures of love will be powerful in the hands of the Holy Spirit.*

- *Transparency and extravagant generosity are marks of the Holy Spirit.*

- *World systems can never bring lasting peace.* Only Jesus can satisfy the soul.

- *Force and manipulation are marks of satanic activity and influence.*

- *Spiritual power and authority rests in humility.*

- *Disillusionment is God's invitation* to spiritual growth.

An Invitation

St. Ignatius taught a technique called the "composition of place" as an easy method for Christians to enter into the scriptural narrative as participants.

Ignatius takes a biblical scene and invites us through our senses to "be" there in our minds: to taste the wine, smell the sweat, hear the crowds, feel the grit, and see the beards. Once we've tried to register in every sense what it might have been like to be present alongside our Lord, we tap into the emotions that Christ or the apostles might have felt: the fear, the joy, the confusion, or the hope. A few months of this sort of thing, and Christianity ceases to be an abstraction—as it too often is, even for faithful believers—and becomes a part of your lived reality.

I hope you'll choose one of the profiles in this chapter and place yourself in the narrative as each of the protagonists and antagonists. Turn back to the pertinent verses, and look up each passage so you have all the information the scriptures give about the situation and circumstances. Using all of your senses, try to imagine everything about the scene, as well as the emotions and thoughts of each participant. I hope you'll do this on a daily basis with the Gospel reading, especially if you do not already have a daily scripture habit, or if you find reading the Bible difficult.

Then, reflect: What did you learn?

God Prompt

In *Unleashed* I told the story of Aunt Betty, my husband's great-aunt by marriage who had a sailor's vocabulary and the attitude to go with it. I could write a whole book on all I learned from that unlikely woman and my relationship with her. She lived more than an hour away, and I took my young son with me to clean her house about once a month for nothing. But I did it because I hated it.

I forced myself to clean for her because it was so distasteful. Not her—I actually grew to love her very much—but the daylong, smelly, dirty drudgery of it. I needed it. I needed the humility of spending money for gas when we didn't have it, of cleaning weeks-old feces out of her carpet, mopping her kitchen floors on my hands and knees, dragging an ancient hundred-pound canister vacuum all over the house in a cloud of cigarette smoke, brushing her dentures while dry heaving and praying to Jesus I wouldn't actually vomit, all because it was the most menial service near to hand, and I needed to stoop very, very low because I am very, very proud.

What was the most significant sentence, idea, or paragraph you read in this chapter? Was there any place that caused a strong reaction of some kind—perhaps longing, perhaps anxiety, or a flash of insight? If anything particularly struck you in this chapter, could it be the voice of God, acting and moving in your heart and life? What small, concrete action in humility can you take to begin crucifying your pride and laying it at Jesus' feet as Mary did?

Talk to God about your tendency to be fake and stingy with others in your life. Do you have a hard time being transparent or generous? Why or why not? Looking back over your life, when were you most like Mary? How are you most like Judas?

Attempt to discern the lie. Being emotional is not negative. Mary is emotional, but she doesn't just have the feeling, this upswell of love. She goes on to do something good about it. The apostles at that dinner were in their heads; she was in her heart. Women have a powerful life-giving relationship with the Holy Spirit. God was using it to give Jesus something he needed to propel him through the next week.

We don't have to defend our gestures to God. Besides Jesus, Mary was the most powerful person in the room. The Holy Spirit was gushing out all over everything. Our strength is the love we give, especially to our families. We hold a position of great power and spiritual authority, but only when we are willing to go as low as we can in giving extravagantly.

Have you begun to understand how Satan uses your natural emotions to control your behavior? What is the lie he whispers into your heart when you are afraid of transparency or generosity?

Probe for the temptation. When are you tempted to be fake with people you consider holier than you? How do you try to use Jesus to further your agenda, rather than allowing him to lead? How do you allow Satan to influence you into resisting God's plan for your life? Why? What about when you were so disillusioned? What do you want to say to Jesus about that?

Let us pray: *Eternal God, in whom mercy is endless and the treasury of compassion inexhaustible, look kindly upon us and increase your mercy in us, that in difficult moments we might not despair or become despondent but with great confidence submit ourselves to your holy will, which is love and mercy itself. For the sake of his sorrowful passion, have mercy on us and on the whole world.*

8

*F*earless Love

A Separate Peace

If learning to love with abandon is the essence of spiritual combat against the enemy and the womb of peace, the Bible gives us no better model than the Son of God who loved his own to the end (Jn 13:1). How do we love our families, our world, our enemy, and our heavenly Father with such total self-gift? How do we throw ourselves completely into the arms of God? How was Jesus able to make the sacrifices he made as a mortal man?

Pope Benedict answers, "Matthew and Luke recount three temptations of Jesus that reflect the inner struggle over his own particular mission and, at the same time, address the question as to what truly matters in human life."[1] The trials the devil puts Jesus to both review and redeem those faced by Adam and Israel in the desert (CCC, 538).

Luminous Mysteries

The first day of Jesus' public ministry begins with thunder. I never pray the Luminous Mysteries without longing to one day hear the words Jesus heard on this day; when wading into the waters of Baptism to bury himself among us common sinners and be consecrated by the Holy Spirit there, he is raised by John the Baptizer into fluttering dove's wings and a disembodied voice: "This is my beloved Son, with whom I am well pleased" (Mt 17:5).

Proving that Baptism and Confirmation are imperative weapons in battle against Satan, theologians say it is the same day, "immediately" following his Baptism, that Jesus is "led" by the Spirit to enter the desert for forty days of fasting, prayer, and temptation (Mt 4:1–11; Mk 1:12–13; Lk 4:1–13). The "forty days" recalls other difficult, prophetic periods of review and preparation in the Old Testament: the forty days and nights of the cleansing deluge (Gn 7:12); the forty days Moses spent on Mt. Sinai with God receiving the Law (Ex 34:28); and the forty years the Israelites wandered through the wilderness in preparation for the Promised Land.

The terms used by the synoptic Gospels[2] to denote being "led" convey a powerful energy in the "leading." Jesus is *impelled, thrust out, borne away,* and *driven* by the Spirit into the desert mountains west of Jericho that are honeycombed with caves, where to this day there stands the ruins of a chapel commemorating Jesus' desolation there.

But for the beasts, Jesus is completely alone in an area otherwise difficult to access (Mk 1:13). It's January, in the middle of a cold, rainy winter, when the trees are bare of fruit or leaves and the sky is low and blustery.

Sharing the same purpose as the other preparatory trials of forty that preceded his own, Jesus will completely clear the way of all obstacles and distractions in the flood of solitude; he will get ready to impart a new law; he will prepare himself to perfectly fulfill Israel's calling and inaugurate the New Israel.

At the end of forty days when he is hungriest and most physically depleted, he will be tempted as the new Adam by the devil, Satan the accuser, who accuses men before God, and God before men, and men before men continually, so he may gain souls for himself and hell.

The devil always offers that which tempts one's weakness, but first he has to discover those particular faults. The sacred writers interpret the approach as an actual, visible, personal attack. And so the temptation commences, in all the ways that a fallen angel's gifts of imagery and eloquence could make attractive to the senses. We should anticipate a respect of sorts in the bait, something super subtle. Satan has been tempting humanity for millennia; surely all his wiles are exerted in discovering who Jesus really is.

Directly after God's public confirmation of his calling and under the compelling influence of the Holy Spirit, Jesus meditated on the principles and relationship that would govern his Messianic vocation in desert solitude. His confrontation with current ideas about the Messianic mission and Jesus' determination of its guiding relationship and principles involved his severest temptation.

The questions and temptations out there in the cold wilderness seem to betray Satan's aim. If Jesus is really the Son of God as was said at his Baptism, what is the nature of his power? Jesus was so absorbed in the endeavor that he refused to eat, so Satan begins his probing as "in the beginning."

198 LOVE WITH ABANDON

Forbidden Food

As we first saw in Eden and later in the wilderness wanderings, natural appetites are a frequent and effective weapon of the devil, as we see in the Gospel of Matthew: "If you are the Son of God, command these stones to become loaves of bread" (4:3).

Remember our theologians conclude from the scriptures that the sin and pride of Lucifer in heaven was the rivalry with which he rebelled when God revealed to the angels that the Son would assume humankind's nature and be elevated above them. Lucifer, the most glorious angel, became insanely jealous of Christ and his divine-human union because he was ambitious for the divine privilege himself.

Having waited millennia for the appearance of the Man whom he would be forced to worship, and upon hearing the mysterious words "Lamb" from John the Baptist and "Son" from God the Father, Satan wishes to find out if he is really the one on whom he has long anticipated pouring out all his malice and violence. But he conceals all this, veiling it behind a facade of helpfulness and concern for Jesus' intense hunger.

Had Jesus turned the rocks into bread as he suggested, the devil would have known absolutely that he was God, and clearly it was not time for that (Lk 4:41). This temptation echoes Adam's power grab for the forbidden fruit and Israel's complaint against Moses for depriving them of the bread they had in Egypt by leading them into the wilderness. Ironically, Jesus would not by a word turn stones into bread for himself, but he will turn bread into his own Body and Blood when the hour has come.

Notice in each case, when Jesus responds to the devil he quotes from Deuteronomy where, through Moses, God took the opportunity to review the Law to prepare the people for their life in the Promised Land. The Law explained the principles and relationship that should guide their living. Jesus knew God allowed their hunger in the desert *in order* that he should provide for them. Hunger was a deliberate test and growth of their faith.

Jesus knows this is also God's plan for his own hunger. In rebuffing the devil, Jesus repeats and brings full circle Moses's rebuke to the Israelites' complaints that he deprived them of the bread they had in Egypt by leading them into the wilderness (Dt 8:3).

I would have run out to Aldi's and put dozens of lemon-filled Krispy Kremes and loaves of pumpernickel on the credit card I'm not supposed to use, but Jesus knows the body cannot nourish the soul. Even more, he understands how feeding the body indiscriminately can impoverish the soul. If man could live by bread alone, surely the majority of the hyperfed Western world would not be depressed. Did you know the Bible says the primary reasons Sodom and Gomorrah were destroyed were pride, gluttony, and laziness, not homosexual activity (Ez 16:49)?

With the first temptation, Satan all but accuses God of neglecting Jesus' hunger and suggests he must provide for himself. Why not? The accusation has worked flawlessly until now.

Ah, but unlike Adam and Eve, unlike the Israelites in the wilderness, Jesus draws from what he knows of his *relationship* with the Father, not from his hunger. Jesus knows and experiences the love in the Father's bosom. Rather than using his power to provide food for himself, Jesus is content to fall back on love, and what he knows from the scriptures, to guide and express how he will respond to his hunger. Unlike impatient me or the complaining Israelites, he entrusts his need for food to God who sustained millions for a whole generation without bread at all. Later in his Sermon on the Mount when he gives the new law, Jesus will teach this very lesson himself when he says, "What man of you, if his son asks him for bread, will give him a stone?" (Mt 7:9).

Besides being hungry, I imagine it might have been an attractive idea to poof those rocks into bread just to shut Satan up. In essence, though (as one saint somewhere said) Jesus was saying, "I'm going to fight and beat you with the hand of my divinity tied behind my back." His humility in waiting and refusing to assert power was what shocked Judas so completely.

Jesus teaches us that "fasting is as wings, whereby the soul is carried upward to celestial things."[3] If you are experiencing spiritual attack or confusion, try adding a fast to your prayer. After forty days of fasting on a cold, bare mountain, just when he should be weakest and most depleted, Jesus is most powerful against the enemy.

Biblical humility is not groveling in a lack of dignity or worth. Jesus' intention to overcome Satan through humility rather than power was simply because that's how the Father does things. Jesus shows us humility is harder than the deprecating portrayal of one's gifts and is much more than a simple awareness of one's limitations. As the Son of God, Jesus possessed infinite dignity and worth and was limited only as he allowed himself to be. Humility, as exemplified in Jesus, is suffering limitation and asking God to provide, resting in God's will that I be inadequate of myself, rather than attempting to be self-sufficient.

When the temptation is, *will I be self-sufficient rather than trust God to provide?* Jesus throws himself on the mercy of his Father and loves with abandon.

Shock and Awe

The first temptation proves Jesus is a man of faith. The second (in St. Matthew's order of presentation) is addressed to him as such, daring him to prove God's care through a test of his own. If he is the Son of God, he should throw himself off the highest point of the Temple in Jerusalem for everyone to see. Since Jesus first responded to him by quoting scripture, the devil now quotes a psalm of his own, a psalm of protection. Psalm 91:11–12 is the basis for the temptation. Again, he says, "*If* you are the Son of God . . ." (Mt 4:6). Then Satan points out that the scriptures say God will deliver those who trust in him. The accusation lurks beneath: if God does not deliver him, he is not his Son.

Once when I was failing to quit smoking, I asked God to help me resist an awful craving I was having *while* I was buying a pack of cigarettes to cheat. Why is this an example of tempting God?

The Bible does say that those who trust in God will receive his protection. It does not condone the presumption of taking reckless risks or insisting on miracles to test whether God will keep his word. Judas tempted Jesus this way in trying to force him to act (*CCC*, 2119), as though the whims of humanity could manipulate God. I distinctly remember that the automatic window on my car inexplicably would not lower, and yet I smoked the cigarette and went back to the habit in the face of that answered prayer.

Jesus did not respond either time to "If you are the Son of God," but Satan knew Jesus was superior somehow since he hadn't fallen to the first temptation; therefore, he probably *was* the Messiah promised to Israel. Now there was only one intention: to manipulate Jesus into revealing himself too soon, and in a way that improperly exposed both his mission and his nature. Satan was probing for information, simultaneously gathering data and striking to win.

With the second suggestion, Satan tempted Jesus to vanity and pride, and greed of greatness, as he formerly had Adam and Eve: "You will be like God" (Gn 3:5). When the devil sees anyone limit the pleasures and allurements of her natural appetites, the Fathers say, he tries the temptation of greatness and presumption. Is it bad, then, to exercise power or to desire honor? It is good, the Fathers point out, if they are bestowed upon us, not if they are seized.

She who asks for a miracle without necessity tempts God, such as this would have been, for Christ could have easily descended from the Temple's pinnacle by way of the stairs. So we see it is demonic to throw ourselves into danger to see if God will rescue us.

Satan, pointing to the crowds thronged in the Temple courts, painted a picture of Jesus floating down, encircled by a fantastic entourage of angels, to rest among the upturned faces of adoring men. Would this not compel their worship and awe? If the Messiah is meant to be famous, then this could not have been more alluring to him, and just to make it irresistible, Satan strengthened the suggestion with scripture.

Jesus recognizes the temptation and quotes Deuteronomy 6:16, in which Moses rebukes the Israelites for having put God to the test in the wilderness. This "testing" is why Jesus was constantly telling people not to tell of his healings and miracles: "He did not come to make a display. He came to heal and to teach suffering men. For one who wanted to make a display the thing would have been just to appear and dazzle the beholders. But for Him Who came to heal and to teach, the way was not merely to dwell here, but to put Himself at the disposal of those who needed Him."[4]

And again, Jesus' lesson later makes it into his teaching repertoire: "This generation is an evil generation; it seeks a sign, but no sign shall be given to it" (Lk 11:29).

One more important point on this temptation: Satan's knowledge of and use of scripture to tempt is the most critical reason the sword of the Spirit is sheathed in the Church of history. The Church is the foundation of truth, not the Bible (1 Tm 3:15), for in the devil's hands, any verse can take on any believable meaning and be used for any evil.

All of us have seen and experienced being clubbed over the head with a Bible verse taken out of context. As the visible Body of Christ, the lamp on the hill, the Church protects and guards the Deposit of Faith and its interpretation from error. How do you know if your interpretation is right when it is contradicted by others you know are as holy or holier than you? Isn't a matter of life or death an important enough reason to know?

When the temptation is, *will I presume on God's love, will I force my "right," will I attempt to be seen, rather than wait on God's leadership to reveal me?* Jesus patiently waits and loves with abandon. Once Satan is defeated on the pinnacle of the Temple, he takes Jesus to the mountain.

Pursuing the Summit

Several years ago when I was in my own desert trial of about three years, in the middle of an extended fast and undergoing the darkest spiritual time of my life to date, my family took a trip to Roane Mountain in east Tennessee to hike and camp a leg of the Appalachian Trail.

I've already shared that during that time God was teaching me rest as a discipline. Unlike Jesus, who knew it while in the wilderness temptations, I realized only in hindsight that on this trip God was giving me a "review" of Deuteronomy and those Old Testament wilderness wanderings in the same way he used them with the Israelites and with Jesus after them: to help me hone my ministry vision and determine relationship principles that would guide my possession of the Promised Land.

While my husband and eight-year-old carried provisions, I packed our infant through the evergreen thicket at the foot of the mountain and up miles of bare switchback trails to the bald, with an atrocious attitude. In my defense, I have often found it necessary to ask forgiveness for things I've said and done in hunger, and I was so hungry at the time—for food, for communion, for warmth, for . . . I had no idea what, just that I was so desolate.

I love hiking, but my soul longs for rest in the mists rising from rushing waters and the swirling exhalations of conifers. I wanted to wallow in the lap of dense forest, with fresh water to cool our feet and sing us to sleep, not bear this cold, unprotected bald hill with only scraggly brush to look at and scads of fine pebbles to trip us all the way up. I assented with my best martyr's face because my husband really wanted to try the hike and the mountain, but I offered up my distaste the whole time.

The only way I know to describe the final experience is "eerie." There were other hikers on the highest peak, so we made camp in the moss covering the side of the next highest, opposite bald. The view was stunning above wave upon wave of mountains (just like the cover of this book), but I began to realize it was like watching television on mute. I didn't notice until we watched several four-wheelers slinging along not far below us without hearing their motors; chirping birds perched on the heather close by but no songs; and crickets and other bugs in the dense moss without sound. I didn't even hear the wind, even though it gusted and tossed the sparse vegetation around us.

I descended that silent, peak metaphor for God's presence into the most intense spiritual Promised Land experience of my life, feeling a lot like God was showing me those peaks in that silence as a promise of things to come.

As Jesus knew, mountains have a way of doing that to you.

In the Shadow of the Most High

Such silent awe on the mountain can hardly be attributed to Lucifer. In this third assault (in Matthew's order), we hear nothing of his rage at being successfully opposed by a lowly man, but surely Jesus' repeated quiet responses pulsed in Satan's ears and the surrounding air like Hiroshima.

In the two previous temptations, Satan examined directly whether Christ was the Son of God, but in this third temptation his object is to thwart his mission. Satan does not ask, *Are you the Son of God?* for there can be no doubt now. And since he is certain, he takes the tack against Jesus that is most likely to succeed, as it had previously felled Lucifer himself, of old: "I will sit on the mount of assembly . . . I will ascend above the heights of the clouds, I will make myself like the Most High" (Is 14:13-14). This was the battle cry of revolt Satan once flung in the face of heaven.

The former tests have proven Jesus is a man of faith and common sense. Surely such a man would take the shortest, easiest road to what is rightfully his. Satan offers a shortcut.

Reflecting the uncontested influence he retained in the world order from Adam to that time, the devil offers Jesus all the earthly kingdoms, illustrated by all those visible from the highest peak, if he will worship him.

Either Satan ignores or is conveniently ignorant of the irony that he has already begun losing them all to Jesus (Rv 11:15). After all, during Jesus' public life we will see Satan groveling at his feet and come to realize that his power is so limited that he is unable even to possess pigs if Jesus does not permit it first (Mk 3:11; Mt 8:29–31). But there is a sense in which this temptation must have been the most powerfully attractive to Jesus.

As a Jewish man, Jesus knew the prophecies regarding the Messiah's universal kingdom inside and out. In fact, we will watch his entire ministry unfold and take flight from the cocoon of the Old Testament worship structure. That it was the will of God according to the scriptures for that kingdom to become a reality would have been clear in Jesus' mind; wasn't it his whole purpose in coming?

Satan must have also known that an observant Jew would shrink from literally prostrating before him. Simple respect for Jesus' intelligence and Satan's superhuman abilities and knowledge demand that we assume he was tempting Jesus in a subtler, more serious capacity. What's really going on here?

Again, we will see Jesus use this lesson in his own teaching as he clarifies the Jewish understanding of worship, later, when he encounters the woman at the well. "But the hour is coming, and now is, when the true worshipers will worship the Father in spirit and truth, for such the Father seeks to worship him" (Jn 4:23). The Jews worshiped the true God indeed, but chiefly by animal sacrifices, and only in one particular place, Jerusalem. All of this was shadow and type of the spiritual worship to come through Christ.

Second, scriptural worship means *to sacrifice, to serve,* and *to obey.* It's not merely bowing down or some other outward "can't I just go to Mass?" or hand-raising singing and preaching. Nor is it an inward "I don't need physical church or organized religion" self-deception. The Jesus we worship and emulate is *both* body *and* spirit, so that spirit-only, invisible worship is as un*true* as outward-only physical worship. True worshipers worship by abandonment to love: sacrificing in obedience to God from a heart of love.

If Satan can offer world domination with all its power, ease, politics, and intrigue, what was this temptation really about? What does Satan want Jesus to do? Is he advocating a warlike political Messiah, one of power and control rather than service? Maybe he is—probably. Maybe Satan is simply asking, *Is that what God is like*?

But what if the temptation is as simple as—dare I say—expedience? What if it's about eliminating the painful waiting, hurtful misunderstandings, arduous difficulties, laborious suffering, and agonizing death of a slow ascent? If you think this and all the temptations weren't attractive to Jesus, think forward to his blood sweat on the eve of his passion.

What kind of kingdom is God capable of offering that Satan can never offer? He can offer one built on love, and wooing a suitor like the human race is slow business. Satan was offering all the earthly glories of a kingdom without the wait, without the innumerable sacrifices. He asks Jesus to play into the false, political understanding of the Messiah's role that was popular at the time. Such a simple compromise would be service to Satan who *will not serve*: worship.

This third temptation echoes Adam's power grab in the Garden, wanting to be like God without the union of purposes and wills, as well as the false worship the Israelites committed in the desert, both at the incident of the Golden Calf (Ex 32:4) and more generally in their refusal to trust God's timing, substance, and leadership provision in the desert.

When the temptation is, *will I compromise by short-cutting, avoiding the sacrifices and suffering necessary to reach the promise, rather than embrace the cross that precedes resurrection?* Jesus lays his will in the Father's hands and loves with abandon.

At the sight of this monster of pride, Jesus banishes the devil by quoting Deuteronomy 6:13, reflecting the fundamental requirement of Israelite worship service: "Then Jesus said to him, 'Begone, Satan! for it is written, "You shall *worship* the Lord your God and him only shall you *serve*"'" (Mt 4:10, emphasis added).

Interestingly, the original Hebrew of Deuteronomy 6:13 is rendered *fear*: "Thou shalt *fear* the Lord thy God, and shalt serve him only, and thou shalt swear by his name" (DRB). This is the *fear of the Lord* that is the gift of the Holy Spirit in Isaiah 11:1–2. For the Jew the word *fear* signifies reverence, service, obedience, and adoration—the whole worship of God. Dear One, what you fear is what you serve, and what you serve is what you worship.

Love Is the Only Fulfillment

Many people—Judas and the other apostles and I too—want a messiah who will seize political power, force his enemies to serve, and usher in an age of prosperity and plenty. But Jesus voluntarily undergoes hunger and refuses contrived spectacles and worldly political power—a very different kind of Messiah.

Jesus' temptation reveals the way in which the Son of God is Messiah, contrary to the way Satan proposes to him and the way men wish to attribute to him. This is why Christ vanquished the tempter for us: "For we have not a high priest who is unable to sympathize with our weaknesses, but one who in every respect has been tempted as we are, yet without sinning" (Heb 4:15).

Satan uses these same perfectly innocent, natural appetites and instincts—physical need, scriptural promises, and legitimate plans and purposes of God—to trap us in sin. In 1 John, we read, "Do not love the world or the things in the world. If anyone loves the world, love for the Father is not in him. For all that is in the world, the lust of the flesh and the lust of the eyes and the pride of life, is not of the Father but is of the world" (1 Jn 2:15–16).

Jesus is not afraid in the desert; he is not anxious. He tells us, "Let not your hearts be troubled, neither let them be afraid" (Jn 14:27). Doesn't Jesus make it sound as though I too can have control over my fear? "Have no anxiety about anything, but in everything by prayer and supplication with thanksgiving let your requests be made known to God. And the peace of God, which passes all understanding, will keep your hearts and your minds in Christ Jesus" (Phil 4:6–7).

Peace is Jesus. He shows us that the way to peace is loving with abandon: resisting self-sufficiency by asking, anticipating, and hoping in God for provision in all our hungers and needs; resisting temptations to presumption and force by submission and obedience to God's timing; and confronting rebellion and pride by embracing the slowness and suffering inherent in our duties and vocation.

The evangelists indicate the salvific meaning of this mysterious event: Jesus is the new Adam who remained faithful just where the first Adam had given in to temptation. Jesus fulfills Israel's vocation perfectly: in contrast to those who had once provoked God during forty years in the desert, Christ reveals himself as God's Servant, totally obedient to the divine will. In this, Jesus is the devil's conqueror: he "binds the strong man" to take back his plunder and he gives it to us! Jesus' victory over the tempter in the desert anticipates victory at the Passion, the supreme act of obedience of his filial love for the Father (CCC, 539).

And then there is calm. Angels serve him. He is unassailable until his hour. Satan will leave him alone but for harassments by the Pharisees and gather his strength until Jesus' anointing in Bethany. There, having found a foothold of ambition in the heart of a beloved disciple, Jesus is betrayed by the suggestion of Satan through one who is closest to him, and the momentum shifts to the zenith of the Passion.

Even on the Cross, when Jesus is hanging in agony of love, Satan will attack Jesus with all the fury of his ancient despair, and his supremely subtle exertion will be leveled at Jesus through those he loves. Betrayed by friends, abandoned and alone, and wearing only Mary's oil, he battles the ultimate desolation of his Father on the Cross, from which he will cry, "My God, my God, why have you forsaken me?" (Mt 27:46), and then once again place his soul in the hands of his Father (Lk 23:46).

Jesus shows us that conquering fear, anxiety, and depression happens from the humility of the Cross.

Let's Review

Before we draw our journey to a close, let's look back at how to conquer our demons and love with abandon as fearless women of God.

- *Fear is not of God* (2 Tm 1:17), but a matter of spiritual warfare (Eph 6:12). Fear is an attack on love (1 Jn 4:18).

- *Sin causes fear, anxiety, and depression. Sin diminishes me*; it makes me weak and vulnerable to demonic suggestion and influence.

- *"To obey is better than sacrifice* . . . for rebellion is as the sin of witchcraft" (1 Sm 15:22–23, NKJV). Satan has no legitimate claim on me. Nothing can separate me from the love of God (Rom 8:38–39).

- *To sin is to believe a lie*. Satan "is a liar and the father of lies" (Jn 8:44).

- *Through the power of Christ, I never have to sin*: "Sin will have no dominion over you, since you are . . . under grace" (Rom 6:14).

- *Reentering a dependent relationship with God begins the renewal* of all that has become disordered and fearful in my life.

- *Satan, meaning "adversary," exploits my woundedness and suffering* with lies to keep me in fear and isolated from love.

- *Satan's lie is that I am unlovable and worthless* unless I do something deserving of love.

- *Rebellion = sin = lies = untrust = unbelief = unrest = fear = evil*

- *The Bible never calls me to fight* on offense against the devil. I am only commanded to stand firm in the armor of God and resist through his Word.

- *God's Word is a principal weapon* in the battle against fear, sin, and temptation: "The word of God is living and active, sharper than any two-edged sword" (Heb 4:12). In him I am more than a conqueror (Rom 8:37).

- *Force, hurry, self-sufficiency, and manipulation are marks of satanic activity* and influence.

- *Spiritual power and authority rests in humility.*

- *Trusting God for all my needs, waiting on him, and submitting to his timing and provision is abandonment to love and the key to fearlessness.*

An Invitation

Sometimes, when immersion for a time in nature; praying; praising; rosaries; relaxation techniques; wine; essential oils; adoration; road trips; silence; redirecting; music; food; journaling; therapy; chocolate; gratitude; medication; workouts; prayers to St. Michael, St. Joseph, and St. Dymphna; meditation; sharing; Confession; dietary changes; detaching; cleaning; talking through it or talking it down; rigorous activity; supplements; contemplation; and Bible verses have not worked (yes folks, I've tried it all), you have to face fear head on.

I'd like to end our study with a tidy little credo that the Bible offers for how to deal with fear, anxiety, and depression. I hope you'll find it helpful enough to pivot to it whenever you're assaulted by fear, because in this story God actually deals with the fear of one of his beloved servants, personally and systematically.

Elijah was one of the greatest prophets in the history of God's people, and he was being pursued by evil. Evil powers wanted him dead, and he knew it. He ran. He hid. The fear found him. He fell into an extended depression, to the point that he was suicidal. But God was with him the whole time. He prepared him to conquer his demons with "the peace that passes understanding" and faced him forward to love with abandon.

We are in a battle. We experience fear. Sometimes it's so strong it takes our breath and leaves us in anguish. According to psychiatrists, serious depression is anger that has been suppressed, unexpressed, or denied: it's anger underground. And anger is a mask for fear and pain. We know that the majority of Americans suffer from serious, clinical depression at some point in their lives, but most never get help; they just fight the battle on their own.

But depression serves a constructive purpose. Beginning as a normal grief response, depression is absolutely necessary for spiritual growth because it's the natural process of letting go of something no longer helpful or useful. If I am experiencing the fear, low mood, and empty feelings of depression, perhaps nothing has gone horribly wrong. What if God is shaking me out of my comfort zone and errors in faith or perception? What if he is inviting me to move forward?

Sure, it's scary and painful—all loss is difficult—but what if, in order for me to grow, God has to disillusion me of unrealistic ideals or expectations and the faith I placed in sin, self, and fallible people and constructions?

The problem arises when depression becomes a rut and we're stuck. Prolonged fear or "sadness chemicals" cause imbalances that we may need professional help to deal with while we work on the relevant issues.

One of God's greatest prophets struggled with fear, anxiety, and depression. Fortunately, God helps us by giving us this case study in 1 Kings 19. We see from the text that Elijah experienced many classic symptoms of fear-induced depression:

- Fear: Elijah was afraid and ran for his life (1 Kgs 19:3).

- Suicidal thoughts: Elijah prayed that he might die (1 Kgs 19:4).

- Excessive sleepiness: "He lay down and slept under a broom tree" for a couple of days or longer (1 Kgs 19:5–7).

- Irritability and feelings of rejection: "I have been very jealous for the LORD, the God of hosts; for the sons of Israel have forsaken your covenant, thrown down your altars, and slain your prophets with the sword; and I, even I only, am left; and they seek my life, to take it away," he says, repeating his complaint twice (1 Kgs 19:10).

Elijah struggled with his depression for nearly two months, well past the recommended length of time for getting help.

What's really bizarre about this is, just days before it started, Elijah preached one of the most powerful sermons of his life and performed astounding miracles to confirm all he said. He confronted four hundred prophets of Baal on Mt. Carmel, exposing them to God's people as the false prophets they were.

In direct response to Elijah's heroic faith and obedience, and against overwhelming odds, God publicly accepted his sacrifice, literally sending fire falling from heaven to consume the sacrifice and confirm Elijah's ministry. A few hours later he sent a downpour of rain on a land that had suffered drought for three years, also in answer to Elijah's prayers.

Why would a man who had just experienced such miraculous, powerful displays of God's affirmation and power suddenly be crippled by fear, hopelessness, and despair? Why would he run to a desolate corner of the world and seek to die? Maybe he did so for the same reason Jesus was driven to the wilderness after hearing the thunder proclaim him "beloved."

Some have called this after-the-mountaintop experience postadrenaline depression and suggested we just cooperate with it, saying that when the adrenal system crashes, its need for rejuvenation far exceeds any need just to feel better. In fact, the mood is deliberately designed to isolate me and slow me down so I can take an internal inventory and recovery can take place. Rather than fighting this feeling, it is best to listen to its message and try to rest. Important matters are sorted out in this low, desolate time.

Not necessarily a lack of faith or indication of sin, then, Elijah's state shows us that God's most dynamic servants sometimes suffer from fear and depression by design. God recognized that Elijah's fear was not an imaginary problem. Elijah's depression was real. It was tangible. You could have cut it with a knife. God did not say, "Get a hold of yourself Elijah. This is a sinful attitude. Where's your faith? You need to pray more and work harder." Elijah was pursued by evil and fear, but that's not where God left him, and he would use it for Elijah's benefit.

Get with God

Elijah ran from the hounds of hell that pursued him to Beersheba, meaning *the well of the covenant*. In answer to Elijah's prayer to die, God just stayed close and let him sleep. God's angel fed him and let him sleep some more. Then God sent him on a journey of forty days and nights to a solitary mountain cave.

In all that time, God didn't say a word—no sermon, no counseling session. God did not treat Elijah roughly. He didn't set Elijah down for a face-to-face talk. God left Elijah alone to rest, think, and regather strength in his presence. But eventually God dealt directly with Elijah's depression in the isolation of that mountain cave.

Get Outside

We know it's true, and Pope Francis emphasized it especially for our times: "We were not meant to be inundated by cement, asphalt, glass and metal, and deprived of physical contact with nature. . . . The entire material universe speaks of God's love, his boundless affection for us. Soil, water, mountains: everything is, as it were, a caress of God."[5] He goes on to say that spending time communing with God in nature is therapeutic. The psalmist agrees; green pastures and still waters restore our souls (Ps 23).

Part of God's prescription for Elijah's fear and anxiety included sending him on a long hike through several hundred miles of countryside solitude. I too have learned to make immersion in nature a regular discipline. When my chest gets tight and I feel unable to draw a deep breath under the stress of my to-do list, a hike or walk outside—alone with the deer, butterfly, daisy, and frog—never fails to return me to myself.

Get to Church

God sent Elijah to Mt. Horeb, the Mountain of God where the Word of the Law was given to Moses, and where Elijah would hear God's still, small voice in the whisper. You might even say God sent Elijah to "church," but the Word of God came to Elijah because Elijah was alone, silent, disposed, desperate, and listening for it.

God speaks directly to us in the scriptures and in the Mass. He feeds us at "the well of the covenant" with his Body and Blood, nourishing, nurturing, and sustaining us with himself, his wholly separate peace and presence. Are we listening for his Word to us?

The interpersonal connections we make with God and others at church have health benefits. Science confirms that attendance at a house of worship is related to lower rates of depression and anxiety. Also, prayer and meditation have been shown to lower the risk of depression and heart disease and improve immune function. Time alone with God in prayer through the scriptures and Bible study is a powerful antidepressant.

Get in the Word

Twice God asked Elijah, "What are you doing here, Eli'jah?" (1 Kgs 19:13). Didn't God know? Of course he knew, but Elijah needed to vocalize and purge the emotion of what was wrong in his life and explain what he thought the problem was. This transparency is the essence of all real prayer. God knows and designed our need to feel heard and understood, so we can go to him to fill that need. And once Elijah vented and got it all off his chest, God dealt with the false beliefs fueling Elijah's fear.

Jesus said, "The truth will make you free" (Jn 8:32). Why is that? Truth frees us because false ideas and false beliefs, especially about God, have power over us and keep us enslaved to fear, anxiety, sin, and depression. Our lives are built on unreality. Instead, "If any of you lacks wisdom, let him ask God, who gives to all men generously and without reproaching, and it will be given him" (Jas 1:5). Wisdom in the scriptures means to have God's perspective, and God promises to give us this perspective if we ask him. Once we see things the way God sees them, we are able to stop resisting what is, and our fear, anger, and depression begin to lose their grip.

But we have to be watching our circumstances, reading the scriptures, and listening for his voice in our daily Bible reading, regular scripture study, and relationships. We have to be in the truth, and *with* the Truth.

Elijah's reply to God revealed the error in Elijah's thinking: Elijah didn't think God was doing anything (1 Kgs 19:14). Hidden in the midst of Elijah's complaint was an accusation: *I've been beating my head against the wall serving you, Lord. And everything seems to just be falling apart around me. What are you doing?*

When I am afraid, I don't think clearly. I feel as though God has abandoned me and isn't doing anything. I have no hope, no confidence, and I don't see God at all. When I am scared or depressed, I need God's perspective.

So God corrects my thinking with truth, just like he did Elijah's: *Elijah—you're not the only one left* (1 Kgs 19:18). God assures Elijah he has been working all along, even though Elijah couldn't see it. God's got it all under control. Elijah is surrounded with God's help.

Get Moving

When God finished his counseling session with Elijah, he was still in a complaining mood, but God tells him he's got a job for him: "Go, return on your way to the wilderness of Damascus; and when you arrive, you shall anoint Haz'ael to be king over Syria; and Je'hu . . . king over Israel; and Eli'sha . . . to be prophet in your place" (1 Kgs 19:15–16). God got Elijah moving.

We know now that exercise is as or more effective than medication in combatting depression. Get moving. Focus on someone else. Get involved in someone else's ministry and life.

Sometimes medication and professional help are necessary to jump-start the healing of anxiety and depression, so reach out for that help if you need it. But also think about how God dealt with Elijah's fear, anxiety, and depression. Go to him and try his prescription:

Get with God,
Get outside,
Get to church,
Get in the Word, and
Get moving.

Go ahead, try it. Cry out to God. At every step, tell him whatever is troubling you. With St. Padre Pio, let's "come out of anxiety, because it is one of the greatest deceivers of true virtue and sound devotion. Don't spend your energies on things that generate worry, anxiety and anguish. Only one thing is necessary: Lift up your spirit and love God."[6]

God Prompt

What was the most important thing you learned or relearned in your *Fearless* study? What does God want you to do now?

Here in the West we are accustomed to having what we want immediately, microwave popcorn and sitcoms that solve problems in thirty minutes. Spiritual battles for growth and healing, however, are complex and messy. It's not merely difficult; we are incapable of conquering our demons and loving with abandon apart from God. Rather than simply working intensely to solve our problems with fear, anxiety, and depression, we can also offer it all up in communion with Christ's sufferings, so that none of it is lost or arbitrary, knowing that negative emotions are a natural part of our growth in holiness.

We have a marvelous, magnificent, brilliant Father who loves and protects us with complete abandon and has provided every means of grace for us to be free of sin, anxiety, depression, and fear. Every day's events are the soil of that growth. So let's rejoice, knowing that our God is able to complete the good work he began in us (Phil 1:6).

Father John Hardon encourages us in battle:

> For those who are seriously trying to remain faithful to God, the devil is unbelievably clever in trying to induce them to worry, to be anxious, to be discouraged and despondent, and if possible, even to drive them to despair. The devil's intentions are obvious. He knows such people too well not to know that he would not succeed by tempting them to obvious sins. What he wants to do, however, is to deceive such persons into

thinking that a faithful Christian life is burdensome or boring or oppressively difficult. The devil wants to deceive such persons into thinking that such a Christian life is oppressive, it is too much.[7]

Hang in there, Dear One! No study on spiritual warfare can provide simple spiritual recipes that result in your never again facing troublesome emotions or temptations. Such recipes are fine for the parish potluck casserole, but fearlessness requires a vital, living, daily relationship with Jesus, and that lies within our power; it's only a prayer away.

Sometimes our fear, anxiety, and depression are so acute and protracted that they require professional intervention as well as daily spiritual work. If you need that help, please reach out. Do not ignore such emotional challenges, because they do not improve with time. You must not feel ashamed, and you must be persistent until you feel you are receiving the help you need. Remember that shame in neediness is a lie of Satan to keep you enslaved. God works to heal and strengthen us through doctors and other professionals too. All growth is spiritual, so seek help from God and others, remembering that's part of reentering the circle of relationship that connects us to God.

God is at work in your fear, anxiety, and depression. Don't judge it to be bad simply because it is difficult or painful work. It's all important work. In fact, being weak and broken is mysteriously essential to experiencing the power of his love and care: "My power is made perfect in weakness" (2 Cor 12:9).

Furthermore, no one elected me the boss of spiritual warfare. I speak for myself here and feel obliged to detail God's approach with me, because he leads me to a separate peace through it. But I do so with no more authority than any other Christian. I circle back through the helps offered here as my fears, anxieties, and bouts of depression arise; you may want to try that too. In the meantime, while we are working out our fears and weeding out our sin, the only thing left to do is pray to God to make the suffering we are going through count eternally as we offer it to him as a sacrifice of love.

Once we have abandoned ourselves to love, we desire nothing but what God wills to send; we accept all things from the Giver without judging "good" and "bad." "He only does wondrous things" (Ps 72:18, NKJV); how could anything filtered through his love ultimately be bad?

The life of mankind is a warfare on earth. It was given us, said St. Hilary, not to spend it in laziness but to wage a continual war against our spiritual enemies. St. Ambrose says when you are tempted, recognize that a crown is being prepared for you: "Take away the contests of the martyrs, you take away their crowns. Take away their torments, you take away their beatitudes."[8]

Dear One, let no one say to you, "What difference does it make?" That's the way the world thinks. For the world, despite all its pretense of love for every individual, considers people to be machines, mere stuff, commodities to be exploited. Do not believe it. Conquering your demons and learning to live and love with abandon makes *all* the difference, for you and for all you have been given. The next person you greet may be on the verge of sainthood or damnation.

Eternity is at stake. Each moral choice we make repeats the drama of Eden. Every one of our yeses prepares us for the restoration of life. Everything you entrust to Jesus will be kept for eternity in him. God forbid we leave anyone or anything he has given us behind, undone, unrealized, or unfulfilled because we are unwilling to "do whatever he tells" us to do to prepare for eternity (Jn 2:5). No one can do everything, but everyone can do battle for all she's been given.

Pope Francis says to begin here: "Drawing near to the Gospel, meditating on it, and incarnating it in daily life is the best way to know Jesus and bring him to others. This is the vocation and the joy of every baptized person: to show and give Jesus to others. But to do this, we have to know him, and have him dwelling within us, as the Lord of our life. And he defends us from evil, from the devil, who is always couching at our door, at our heart, wanting to enter."[9]

In the end, the one thing necessary to conquer our demons and love with abandon is Jesus. In Jesus, I am fearless.

Group Facilitator Guide

Whether this is the first time you have ever led a group study, or if it is just the first time you're reading *Fearless* and you'd like to put a group together, here are a few suggestions to get you started.

What Is the Job of a Facilitator?

The beauty of this format is that the only requirement needed to facilitate a *Fearless* group study is a willingness to facilitate and a desire to help others draw closer to God through the scriptures. The most important element in the success of your group will be your own commitment to Christ and the weekly reading and exercises.

Depending on the needs of your group, many facilitators also provide some kind of administrative leadership for the group by

- scheduling, promoting, and coordinating the *Fearless* group study;
- ordering books, and DVDs (available at Amazon and biblestudyevangelista.com) should you choose to include the videos in your study;
- distributing books to participants;
- greeting, encouraging, and communicating with participants;
- guiding (and sometimes charitably limiting) group discussion;
- facilitating prayer intentions and group prayers;
- arranging for simple refreshments or other forms of hospitality; and

- encouraging participants to complete the reading and exercises before each class.

How to Lead the Group Study

After receiving the books, take a few minutes to look through your own to familiarize yourself with its format before distributing and introducing copies to the other participants. Each participant should have his or her own copy of *Fearless* as well as a Catholic Bible such as the *Revised Standard Version: Catholic Edition* or the *New American Bible*.

The book's eight chapters divide easily into eight weeks of group discussion lasting forty-five minutes to one hour. You may also wish to add an introductory week at the beginning of the study for administering information on restroom and other facilities, introductions, passing out books, pointing out the special features of each chapter, and discussing the introductory questions provided at the end of that section. They can be answered without having read a word of the book and will help launch participants into their individual reading. The introductory week is the perfect time for the facilitator to recommend that each member bring her Bible to every meeting, as you will be using them a lot.

Supplementary DVDs

A subject as deep and wide as spiritual warfare is difficult to cover sufficiently in eight chapters or even eight volumes; paring down to the basic tenets in this book left a lot of important material neglected. Therefore, a supplemental set of DVDs is available for purchase online at Amazon or biblestudyevangelista.com. Produced for television, the set includes thirteen thirty-minute episodes containing all-new, complementary teaching not included in the book. They are not necessary to do the study, but they definitely contribute toward a more complete understanding and practice of biblical spiritual warfare, as you will see by the additional topics included in the episode guide below. You and your group may choose to do two videos at each of the several study weeks, or you may choose to draw the study out to thirteen weeks. Here is a helpful episode guide to assist you in deciding whether to include the DVDs in your study:

1. Let There Be Light: The Word as Weapon

2. The New Adam and the New Eve

3. LIVEVIL: Revenge and Unforgiveness

4. The Way of Cain: Dealing with Anger

5. The Error of Balaam: Greed and False Profits

6. The Rebellion of Korah: Recognizing Rebellion

7. End-Times Prophecy from a Church History Perspective

8. Leviathan: Evil Influences in Political and Economic Institutions

9. Judas and the Valley of Hell

10. A Study of Job: Learning to Suffer with Dignity

11. Hair, Glory, and Spiritual Influence

12. Sing with the Cherubim: Offering Sacrificial Praise

13. Preview of *Ignite: Unlock the Riches of Scripture and Rejuvenate your Faith*, by Sonja Corbitt and Deacon Harold Burke-Sivers

Each group meeting might look like this: begin with prayer; welcome participants; make introductions, if needed; answer and discuss the questions for the chapter; watch the DVD; facilitate discussion; provide closing prayer; and receive prayer requests and intentions.

You may get to all the questions provided for the chapter each week, and you may not. Some fellowship groups like to offer food and beverages; some don't. Some groups want to conserve discussion time by collecting prayer intentions on slips of paper at the beginning and having each person take one home to pray over for the week. Depending on the personality of your group, you may do more eating, fellowshipping, and general discussion than discussing every question for every chapter. That's fine.

Can Participants Come to Class If They Haven't Done the Reading Each Week?

I hope every group facilitator will challenge and encourage participants to *do* the session heart-work each week. Maybe your women will want to track their progress in a journal; maybe they'll prefer to write in their books. But each chapter's heart-work is short enough that it should always be finished.

Because we are all way too busy, you will inevitably run across those who come to community meetings without their Invitation and God Prompt sections completed. Participants who have not completed the heart-work should still be encouraged to come, because they will get a lot out of the group discussion. Still, there is no substitute for an engaged participant. I hope you will not only pray for each of your participants but also encourage them to complete each chapter, since each one gets them immediately in touch with God in the scriptures.

How to Facilitate a Good Discussion

Creating a welcoming environment is important. Make sure there are enough seats for everyone in the group, and consider arranging seating facing one another in a circle or other inclusive way.

When it's time to pray together, try to guide prayer intentions and sharing so that everyone who wants to is able to participate, but do so without pushing participants to respond or share. Nurture this fellowship between the study participants, as it is a great help to learning and feeling as though one is an integral part of the universal Church.

In almost every group there will be a participant who dominates the discussion. You may need to limit this person's comments as charitably as possible, for the benefit of the whole group and time constraints.

Be enthusiastic, but always start and finish on time, helping the last person speaking to reach a point of conclusion if necessary. Follow up with participants if you discern a particular need.

Finally, this book is about learning from the Holy Spirit how to conquer our demons and love with abandon. Depend on him. You are the facilitator. Your main job is to facilitate sharing and discussion in a way that sets boundaries but is also sensitive to the leading of the Holy Spirit in his people. He has called you to this task, and he is personally involved in both you and your study group. I'm just a Facebook "like" away; let's get in touch. Blessings, friend!

Notes

Introduction

1. My predominant fault is my prevailing sin pattern, a defect intimately connected to my personality and temperament that influences all my spiritual, mental, emotional, and even physical faculties. See Sonja Corbitt, *Unleashed: How to Receive Everything the Holy Spirit Wants to Give You* (Notre Dame, IN: Ave Maria Press, 2015), 46.

2. Jorge Bergoglio, *On Heaven and Earth: Pope Francis on Faith, Family, and the Church in the Twenty-First Century* (New York: Image, 2013), 9.

3. John Paul II, "Apostolic Visit of His Holiness John Paul II to Azerbaijan and Bulgaria: Pilgrimage to the Holy Monastery of Rila," Holy See, May 25, 2002, accessed January 5, 2016, http://w2.vatican.va/.

4. Julian of Norwich, *Revelation of Love* (New York: Image Books, 1996), 55.

5. *Fearless* DVDs are available at Amazon.com or http://biblestudyevangelista.com. An episode guide is provided in the back of this book.

1. A Fearless Battle

1. Bergoglio, *On Heaven and Earth*, 8.

2. For a discussion of the "fear of the Lord" as a gift of the Holy Spirit, see Thomas Aquinas, "Question 19: The Gift of Fear" (*Summa Theologica*, Secunda Secundae Partis, Q. 19), New Advent, 2008, accessed March 7, 2016, http://www.newadvent.org/.

3. Charles Warren Stoddard, *Saint Anthony: The Wonder Worker of Padua* (Rockford, IL: Tan Books, 2009), 58.

4. "The New Rite of Exorcism Is Ineffective against the Evil One" (interview with Gabriele Amorth), *30 Days* (June 2000), accessed January 5, 2016, http://www.fisheaters.com/.

5. Bergoglio, *On Heaven and Earth*, 8.

6. John Paul II, "Apostolic Visit of His Holiness Pope John Paul II to Azerbaijan and Bulgaria."

7. Attributed to St. Augustine in William Sloane Coffin, *The Heart Is a Little to the Left: Essays on Public Morality* (Lebanon, NH: University Press of New England, 1999), 57.

8. Sun Tzu, *The Art of War* (Boston: Shambhala Publications, 2000), 23.

9. Joseph Cardinal Ratzinger, *The Ratzinger Report: An Exclusive Interview on the State of the Church* (San Francisco: Ignatius Press, 1985), 138.

10. Thomas Aquinas, "Question 61: The Production of the Angels in the Order of Natural Being" (*Summa Theologica*, Prima Pars, Q. 61), New Advent, 2008, accessed January 4, 2016, http://www.newadvent.org/.

11. Chad Ripperger, *Introduction to the Science of Mental Health* (Denton, NE: Sensus Traditionis Press, 2013), 535.

12. John A. Hardon, "Father John A. Hardon, S.J., Archives: Demonology; The Strategy of the Devil in Demonic Temptations," Real Presence Association, 1996, accessed January 4, 2016, http://www.therealpresence.org/.

13. C. Bernard Ruffin, *Padre Pio: The True Story* (Huntington, IN: Our Sunday Visitor, 1991), 141, 367.

14. Ratzinger, *Ratzinger Report*, 138.

15. Augustine, *Handbook on Faith, Hope, and Love*, chaps. 8, 27, Christian Classics Ethereal Library, accessed January 5, 2016, http://www.ccel.org/.

16. Job 38:7 taken from "The Greek Old Testament (Septuagint)," Elpinor, accessed January 5, 2016, http://www.ellopos.net/.

17. "Devil," in *The Catholic Encyclopedia*, vol. 4 (New York: Appleton, 1908), New Advent, accessed January 5, 2016, http://www.newadvent.org/.

18. Bergoglio, *On Heaven and Earth*, 8.

19. Bridget of Sweden, *The Revelations of Birgitta of Sweden*, vol. 2 (New York: Oxford University Press, 2008), 277.

20. Thomas Aquinas, "Question 62: The Perfection of the Angels in the Order of Grace and of Glory" (*Summa Theologica*, Prima Pars, Q. 62), New Advent, 2008, accessed January 5, 2016, http://www.newadvent.org/; Thomas Aquinas, "Question 63: The Malice of the Angels with Regard to Sin" (*Summa Theologica*, Prima Pars, Q. 63), New Advent, 2008, accessed January 5, 2016, http://www.newadvent.org/.

21. Thomas Aquinas, "Question 58: The Mode of Angelic Knowledge" (*Summa Theologica*, Prima Pars, Q. 58), New Advent, 2008, accessed January 5, 2016, http://www.newadvent.org/.

22. Paul VI, *Gaudium Et Spes*, Holy See, December 7, 1965, 22, accessed January 5, 2016, http://www.vatican.va/archive/hist_councils/ii_vatican_council/documents/vat-ii_const_19651207_gaudium-et-spes_en.html.

23. Thomas Aquinas, "Question 63: The Malice of the Angels with Regard to Sin" (*Summa Theologica*, Prima Pars, Q. 63), New Advent, 2008, accessed January 17, 2016, http://www.newadvent.org/.

24. Ibid.

25. Attributed to St. Augustine in Coffin, *The Heart*, 57.

26. Sun Tzu, *Art of War*, 23.

27. John Paul II, "Apostolic Visit of His Holiness Pope John Paul II to Azerbaijan and Bulgaria."

28. Ratzinger, *Ratzinger Report*, 138.

29. John A. Hardon, *The Modern Catholic Dictionary* (Bardstown, KY: Eternal Life, 2004), 230.

30. Hardon, "Father John A. Hardon, S.J., Archives: Demonology."

31. Pio of Pietrelcina, "Spiritual Counsels of Padre Pio," Servants of the Pierced Hearts of Jesus and Mary, 2016, accessed March 28, 2016, http:// piercedhearts.org/.

32. Tertullian, *On Baptism*, chap. 3, Christian Classics Ethereal Library, accessed April 29, 2016, http://www.ccel.org/.

33. Gabriel Amorth, *An Exorcist Tells His Story* (San Francisco: Ignatius Press, 1999), 86.

34. Pio, "Spiritual Counsels." Pio is quoting Romans 14:11.

35. Edward Pentin, "Pope Addresses Challenge of Utilizing Mass Media," *National Catholic Register*, March 7, 2005, accessed January 7, 2016, http://www.ncregister.com/.

36. Amorth, *An Exorcist Tells His Story*, 67.

2. Fearless Reconnaissance

1. Leticia Adams, "Sometimes I Leave God Behind to Follow Myself," *Through Broken Roses* (blog), July 24, 2013, accessed March 7, 2016, http:// www.patheos.com/.

2. John Milton, *Paradise Lost* (New York: Norton, 2004), bk. 6, 72.

3. John Paul II, *The Theology of the Body* (Boston: Daughters of St. Paul, 1997), 49.

4. Milton, *Paradise Lost*, bk. 9, 263.

5. "'It is not good for man to be alone: let us make him a helper fit for him'" (Gen 2:18). God entrusted the human being to woman. Certainly, every human being is entrusted to each and every other human being, but in a special way the human being is entrusted to woman, precisely because the woman in virtue of her special experience of motherhood is seen to have a specific sensitivity towards the human person and all that constitutes the individual's true welfare, beginning with the fundamental value of life. How great are the possibilities and responsibilities of woman in this area, at a time when the development of science and technology is not always inspired and measured by true wisdom, with the inevitable risk of 'de-humanizing' human life, above all when it would demand a more intense love and a more generous acceptance." John Paul II, *Christifideles Laici*, 51, Holy See, December 30, 1988, accessed March 7, 2016, http:// w2.vatican.va/content/john-paul-ii/en/apost_exhortations/documents/ hf_jp-ii_exh_30121988_christifideles-laici.html.

6. The language roots are not always obvious, but musical instruments are said to have been "prepared" in Lucifer "on the day" he was created, as indicated by the terms "settings" and "engravings" in Ez 28:13.

7. Milton, *Paradise Lost*, bk. 09, 80.

8. Heather King, *Poor Baby: A Child of the 60's Looks Back on Abortion* (Lexington, KY: CreateSpace Independent Publishing Platform, 2012), 19, Kindle edition.

9. Francis, *Laudato Si'*, Holy See, May 24, 2015, accessed April 30, 2016, http://w2.vatican.va/.

10. Quoted in Alphonsus Liguori, *Sermons of St. Alphonsus Liguori* (Charlotte, NC: TAN Books, 1982), 138.

11. George A. Maloney, *Pseudo-Marcarius: The Fifty Spiritual Homilies* (Mahwah, NJ: Paulist Press, 1992), homily 12.7, 132.

12. Ripperger, *Introduction to the Science*, 353.

13. Ibid., 340.

14. Francis, *Laudato Si'*.

15. See Corbitt, *Unleashed*, chap. 3, and episodes 3 and 4 on the *Fearless* DVDs for more information on rage.

16. Augustine, "On the Trinity (Book XII)," 12:12, New Advent, 2009, accessed March 15, 2016, http://www.newadvent.org/.

17. Ibid.

18. See Corbitt, *Unleashed*, chap. 3.

19. Thomas Aquinas, "Question 35: Sloth" (*Summa Theologica*, Secunda Secundae Partis, Q. 35), New Advent, 2008, accessed May 2, 2016, http://www.newadvent.org/.

20. Attributed to St. Gregory in George Haydock, *Douay Rheims Old Testament of the Holy Catholic Bible with Comprehensive Catholic Commentary* (Moravia, CA: Catholic Treasures 1992), Gn 3:15.

3. Fearless Reinforcement

1. Corbitt, *Unleashed*. See chapter 1, particularly, for discussion on patterns.

2. Catholic Church, "Paschal Vigil Mass *Exsultet*," in *Liber Usualis* (Tournai, Belgium: Desclee, 1961), 776N.

3. Flannery O'Connor, *Mystery and Manners: Occasional Prose* (New York: Farrar, Straus, and Giroux, 2000), 146.

4. C. S. Lewis, *The Great Divorce* (New York: Harper One, 2000), viii.

5. John Paul II, *Christifideles Laici*.

6. Edith Stein, *Woman* (Washington, DC: ICS Publications, 1996), 64.

7. Ibid., 65.

8. "For there is no authority except from God, and those that exist have been instituted by God. Therefore he who resists the authorities resists what God has appointed, and those who resist will incur judgment" (Rom 13:1–2). "Behold, to obey is better than sacrifice . . . for rebellion is as the sin of divination [witchcraft], and stubbornness is as iniquity and idolatry" (1 Sm 15:22–23).

9. Adapted from Heather King's brilliant back-and-forth in *Poor Baby*, 13.

10. "20 Memorable One-Liners from Mother Angelica," Aleteia, March 11, 2016, accessed March 17, 2016, http://aleteia. org/2016/03/11/20-memorable-one-liners-from-mother-angelica/.

4. Fearless Dignity

1. Thomas Aquinas, "Question 3: The Simplicity of God" (*Summa Theologica*, Prima Pars, Q. 3), New Advent, 2008, accessed January 17, 2016, http://www.newadvent.org/.

2. John Henry Newman, "Meditation of the Day," Morning Offerings, February 14, 2016, accessed March 17, 2016, https://www.catholiccompany.com/.

3. Malachi Martin, *Hostage to the Devil* (San Francisco: HarperSanFrancisco, 1992), 389.

4. Thomas Aquinas, "Question 5: Goodness in General" (*Summa Theologica*, Prima Pars, Q. 5), New Advent, 2008, accessed January 17, 2016, http://www.newadvent.org/.

5. Ibid.

6. Reginald Garrigou-Lagrange, *Three Ages of the Interior Life*, vol. 1 (Rockford, IL: Tan Books, 1989), 316.

7. Julian of Norwich, *Revelation of Love*, 79.

8. Civilla D. Martin, "His Eye Is on the Sparrow," 1905. *Library. Timelesstruths.Org*, accessed April 28 2016, http://library.timelesstruths. org/.

9. See Corbitt, *Unleashed*, chap. 3.

10. Martin, "His Eye Is on the Sparrow."

5. A Fearless Desert

1. Talmud, Rashi, Bamidbar 11:7, from Chabad.org, accessed January 18, 2016, http://www.chabad.org/.

2. Joseph Ratzinger, *Jesus of Nazareth* (New York: Doubleday, 2007), 154.

3. Sonja Corbitt, *Bible Study Evangelista*, http://www.biblestudy evangelista.com.

4. Quoted in Cornelius Lapide, *The Great Commentary of Cornelius a Lapide* (Edinburgh: J. Grant, 1908), 1 Corinthians 10:4, e-Sword version.

5. Ibid.

6. *The Lord of the Rings: The Fellowship of the Ring*, directed by Peter Jackson (Wellington, New Zealand: WingNut Films, 2001), DVD.

7. "Coturnism," *Wikipedia*, last updated March 7, 2016, https:// en.wikipedia.org/.

8. See episode 3 of the *Fearless* DVDs.

9. Ripperger, *Introduction to the Science*, 55.

10. 4Him, "Sacred Hideaway," on *The Message* (Benson Records, 1996).

11. Attributed to St. Augustine in Benedict XVI, "General Audience," Holy See, March 9, 2011, accessed April 28, 2016, http://w2.vatican.va/.

6. Fearless Resistance

1. "Bread and circuses" is a phrase coined by a Roman poet in the first century to denote the appeasement of the masses by political classes through a steady diet of diversions, entertainment, and distractions. It was said that the Romans used "bread and circuses" as a palliative for the people.

2. Jean-Pierre de Caussade, *Abandonment to Divine Providence* (New York: Image, 1975), 36, 49.

3. Ratzinger, *Ratzinger Report*, 139.

4. See my radio show on Breadbox Media for a more complete discussion on what faith is and isn't: "What Is Faith?" *Bible Study Evangelista*, January 9, 2016, http://biblestudyevangelista.com/doodah.

5. Ripperger, *Introduction to the Science*, 342–45.

6. C. S. Lewis, *The Screwtape Letters*, annotated ed. (New York: HarperOne, 1996), 64.

7. The earliest reference to contraception and abortion is in the Didache or The Teaching of the Twelve Apostles, a document from the second half of the first century or early second century. The Didache reads, "You shall not practice birth control, you shall not murder a child by abortion, nor kill what is begotten." The complete text is widely available online. Please also research natural family planning.

8. See also the *Manual for Spiritual Warfare*, by Dr. Thomas Paul Thigpen, for further resources along this line (Charlotte, NC: Tan Books, 2014).

9. Mother Teresa, *Come Be My Light* (New York: Doubleday, 2007), 34.

10. Pope Paul VI, "The Word of God: Dei Verbum," Holy See, November 18, 1965, accessed April 29, 2016. http://www.vatican.va/.

11. Bernard of Clairvaux, *Commentary on the Song of Songs*, sermon 23, 3, Internet Archive, accessed May 2, 2016, https://archive.org/.

12. Information on the book *Using the Sword of the Lord* and a handy-dandy booklet that Betty and her friends made illustrating the armor-of-God movements are available on my website, http://www.biblestudyevangelista.com.

7. Fearless Transparency

1. Paul Carlisle, "With All My Heart" (Nashville, TN: Lifeway Press, 2000), 12.

2. Jim Forest, "What I Learned About Justice from Dorothy Day," Clarentian Publications, 1996, accessed January 19, 2016, http://salt.claretianpubs.org/.

3. Benedict XVI, "Magnificat," address given on Monday of Holy Week, Yonkers, NY, 2016.

4. Quoted in Cornelius Lapide, *The Great Commentary of Cornelius*, Jn 12.

5. Ratzinger, *Jesus of Nazareth*, 28.

6. "False humility is very dangerous. Since all virtues are founded on humility, if a person falsifies humility, he cannot attain any other virtue. This is why the demons like it so much." Ripperger, *Introduction to the Science*, 567.

7. Fulton J. Sheen, *Life of Christ* (New York: Image Books, 1958), 257.

8. Mark Shea, "Dealing with Disillusionment," m.ncregister.com, 2016, accessed July 22, 2016, http://m.ncregister.com/.

8. Fearless Love

1. Ratzinger, *Jesus of Nazareth*, 28.

2. The synoptic Gospels are the first three, which are similar in style, sequence, and content.

3. Lapide, *Great Commentary of Cornelius*, Mt. 4:4.

4. Athanasius, *On the Incarnation of the Word*, chap. 7, 43, Christian Classics Ethereal Library, accessed May 2, 2016, http://www.ccel.org/.

5. Francis, *Laudato Si'*, May 24, 2015.

6. Pio, "Spiritual Counsels."

7. Hardon, "Father John A. Hardon, S.J. Archives: Demonology."

8. Quoted in Lapide, *Great Commentary*, Matthew 4.

9. "Pope Francis: Angelus Saint Peter's Square," Jubilee of Mercy, January 3, 2016, accessed March 28, 2016, http://www.im.va/.

Sonja Corbitt is a dynamic Catholic author, speaker, and radio host who has produced several high-impact, uplifting multimedia Bible studies, including *Unleashed, Soul of the World, Fearless,* and *Ignite.*

A Carolina native who was raised as a Southern Baptist, Corbitt attended Mitchell College and the Southern Baptist Seminary Extension and then converted to Catholicism. Corbitt served as director of religious education at St. John Vianney Catholic Church in Gallatin, Tennessee, and as executive director of Risen Radio in Lebanon, Tennessee.

She is the host of *Bible Study Evangelista* on Breadbox Media. Corbitt is in formation as a Third Order Carmelite, a columnist at *The Great Adventure Bible Study* blog, a contributor to *Magnificat,* and the author of *Unleashed.* Her Bible study, *Unleashed,* was featured as a thirteen-part series on CatholicTV. A frequent guest on Catholic radio and television, she also wrote for the *Gallatin News Examiner* and *Oremus,* the Westminster Cathedral magazine. She lives in Tennessee with her husband, Bob, and two sons.

fearless

DVD Series Out Now!

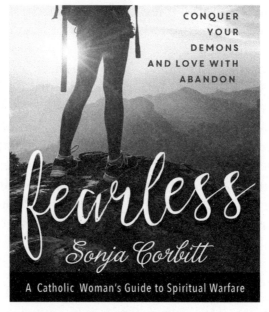

CONQUER YOUR DEMONS AND LOVE WITH ABANDON

fearless

Sonja Corbitt

A Catholic Woman's Guide to Spiritual Warfare

Each 30-minute video in the *Fearless* DVD series offers more teaching and information on spiritual warfare in the scriptures with Sonja.

Order at biblestudyevangelista.com or Amazon.com.

Sonja Corbitt
bible study evangelista.com